SQL Server Internals: In-Memory OLTP

Inside the SQL Server 2014 Hekaton Engine

By Kalen Delaney

Foreword by David DeWitt

Technical Review by Dave Ballantyne

Technical Edit by Tony Davis

First published by Simple Talk Publishing, 2014

Cover Image: Andy Martin
Typeset: Peter Woodhouse and Gower Associates

Table of Contents

Foreword

By David J. DeWitt
Microsoft Technical Fellow
Director, Jim Gray Systems Lab, Madison WI
John P. Morgridge Professor of Computer Sciences, Emeritus
University of Wisconsin-Madison

In-memory OLTP is a game changer for relational databases, and OLTP systems in particular. Processors are not getting faster, but the number of cores and the amount of memory is increasing drastically. Machines with terabytes of memory are available for under $100K. A new technology is needed to take advantage of the changing hardware landscape, and Microsoft's In-Memory OLTP, codenamed Project Hekaton, is that new technology.

Project Hekaton gives us an entirely new way to store and access our relational data, using lock- and latch-free data structures that allow completely non-blocking data processing operations. Everything you knew about how your SQL Server data is actually stored and accessed is different in Hekaton. Everything you understood about how multiple concurrent processes are handled needs to be reconsidered. All of your planning for when code is recompiled and reused can be re-evaluated if you choose to use natively compiled stored procedures to access your Hekaton data.

One of the best things about using this new technology is that it is not all or nothing. Even if much of your processing is not OLTP, even if your total system memory is nowhere near the terabyte range, you can choose one or more critical tables to migrate to the new in-memory structures. You can choose one frequently run stored procedure to recreate as a natively compiled procedure. And you can see measurable performance improvements.

A lot of people are already writing and speaking about in-memory OLTP, on blog posts and in conference sessions. People are using it and sharing what they've learned. For those of you who want to know the complete picture about how in-memory OLTP works and why exactly it's a game changer, and also peek at the deep details of how the data is stored and managed, this book is for you, all in one place. Kalen Delaney has been writing about SQL Server internals, explaining how things work inside the engine, for over 20 years. She started working with the Hekaton team at Microsoft over two years ago, getting the inside scoop from the people who implemented this new technology. And in this book, she's sharing it all with you.

About the Author

Kalen Delaney has been working with SQL Server since 1987, and provides advanced SQL Server training to clients worldwide. She has been a SQL Server MVP since 1993 and has been writing about SQL Server almost as long. Kalen has spoken at dozens of technical conferences, including almost every PASS conference in the US since the organization's founding in 1999. Kalen is the author or co-author of many books on SQL Server, including *SQL Server 2012 Internals*, from Microsoft Press.

She is one of the main editors for SQL Server Central's SQL Server Stairways Series, HTTP://WWW.SQLSERVERCENTRAL.COM/STAIRWAY. Kalen blogs at WWW.SQLBLOG.COM and her personal website and schedule can be found at WWW.SQLSERVERINTERNALS.COM.

Acknowledgements

First of all, I would like to thank Kevin Liu of Microsoft, who brought me on board with the Hekaton project at the end of 2012, with the goal of providing in-depth white papers describing this exciting new technology. Under Kevin's guidance, I wrote two white papers, which were published near the release date at each of the CTPs for

SQL Server 2014. As the paper got longer with each release, a new white paper for the final released project would be as long as a book. So, with Kevin's encouragement, it became the book that you are now reading.

I would also like to thank my devoted reviewers and question answerers at Microsoft, without whom this work would have taken much longer: Sunil Agarwal, Jos de Bruijn, and Mike Zwilling were always quick to respond and were very thorough in answering my sometimes seemingly endless questions.

Others on the SQL Server team who also generously provided answers and/or technical edits include Kevin Farlee, Craig Freedman, Mike Weiner, Cristian Diaconu, Pooja Harjani, Paul Larson, and David Schwartz. Thank you for all your assistance and support. And THANK YOU to the entire SQL Server Team at Microsoft for giving us this incredible new technology!

About the Technical Reviewer

Dave Ballantyne works as a SQL Server data architect for Win Technologies, part of the BetWay group, and lives near London, England. He is a regular speaker at UK and European events and user groups and currently supports the London SQL community by organizing the "SQL Supper" user group. He takes a keen interest in all things SQL and data related, and is never happier than when picking apart a poorly executing query. He has also created an open sourced add-in for SQL Server data tools (SSDT) called *TSQL Smells*. This detects and reports on "suspect" code within a project and can be found at HTTP://TSQLSMELLSSSDT.CODEPLEX.COM.

Outside of work he is husband, father of three, and exasperated archer.

INTRODUCTION

The original design of the SQL Server engine assumed that main memory was very expensive, and so data needed to reside on disk except when it was actually needed for processing. However, over the past thirty years, the sustained fulfillment of Moore's Law, predicting that computing power will double year on year, has rendered this assumption largely invalid.

Moore's law has had a dramatic impact on the availability and affordability of both large amounts of memory and multiple-core processing power. Today one can buy a server with 32 cores and 1 TB of memory for under $50K. Looking further ahead, it's entirely possible that in a few years we'll be able to build distributed DRAM-based systems with capacities of 1–10 Petabytes at a cost of less than $5/GB. It is also only a question of time before non-volatile RAM becomes viable as main-memory storage.

At the same time, the near-ubiquity of 64-bit architectures removes the previous 4 GB limit on "addressable" memory and means that SQL Server has, in theory, near-limitless amounts of memory at its disposal. This has helped to significantly drive down latency time for read operations, simply because we can fit so much more data in memory. For example, many, if not most, of the OLTP databases in production can fit entirely in 1 TB. Even for the largest financial, online retail and airline reservation systems, with databases between 500 GB and 5 TB in size, the performance-sensitive working dataset, i.e. the "hot" data pages, is significantly smaller and could reside entirely in memory.

However, the fact remains that the traditional SQL Server engine is optimized for disk-based storage, for reading specific 8 KB data pages into memory for processing, and writing specific 8 KB data pages back out to disk after data modification, having first "hardened" the changes to disk in the transaction log. Reading and writing 8 KB data pages from and to disk can generate a lot of random I/O and incurs a higher latency cost.

In fact, given the amount of data we can fit in memory, and the high number of cores available to process it, the end result has been that most current SQL Server systems are I/O bound. In other words, the I/O subsystem struggles to "keep up," and many organizations sink huge sums of money into the hardware that they hope will improve write latency. Even when the data is in the buffer cache, SQL Server is architected to assume that it is not, which leads to inefficient CPU usage, with latching and spinlocks. Assuming all, or most, of the data will need to be read from disk also leads to unrealistic cost estimations for the possible query plans and a potential for not being able to determine which plans will really perform best.

As a result of these trends, and the limitations of traditional disk-based storage structures, the SQL Server team at Microsoft began building a database engine optimized for large main memories and many-core CPUs, driven by the recognition that systems designed for a particular class of workload can frequently outperform more general purpose systems by a factor of ten or more. Most specialized systems, including those for CEP (complex event processing), DW/BI and OLTP, optimize data structures and algorithms by focusing on in-memory structures.

The team set about building a specialized database engine specifically for in-memory workloads, which could be tuned just for those workloads. The original concept was proposed at the end of 2008, envisioning a relational database engine that was 100 times faster than the existing SQL Server engine. In fact, the codename for this feature, Hekaton, comes from the Greek word hekaton (ἑκατόν) meaning 100.

Serious planning and design began in 2010, and product development began in 2011. At that time, the team did not know whether the current SQL Server could support this new concept, and the original vision was that it might be a separate product. Fortunately, it soon became evident that, although the framework could support building stand-alone processors (discussion of the framework is well beyond the scope of this book), it would be possible incorporate the "in-memory" processing engine into SQL Server itself.

The team then established four main goals as the foundation for further design and planning:

1. Optimized for data that was stored completely in-memory but was also durable on SQL Server restarts.

2. Fully integrated into the existing SQL Server engine.

3. Very high performance for OLTP operations.

4. Architected for modern CPUs (e.g. use of complex atomic instructions).

SQL Server In-Memory OLTP, formerly known and loved as Hekaton, meets all of these goals, and in this book you will learn how it meets them. The focus will be on the features that allow high performance for OLTP operations. As well as eliminating read latency, since the data will always be in memory, fundamental changes to the memory-optimized versions of tables and indexes, as well as changes to the logging mechanism, mean that in-memory OLTP also offers greatly reduced latency when writing to disk.

The first four chapters of the book offer a basic overview of how the technology works (Chapter 1), how to create in-memory databases and tables (Chapter 2), the basics of row versioning and the new multi-version concurrency control model (Chapter 3), and how memory-optimized tables and their indexes store data (Chapter 4).

Chapters in the latter half of the book focus on how the new in-memory engine delivers the required performance boost, while still ensuring transactional consistency (ACID compliance). In order to deliver on performance, the SQL Server team realized they had to address some significant performance bottlenecks. Two major bottlenecks were the traditional locking and latching mechanisms: if the new in-memory OTLP engine retained these mechanisms, with the waiting and possible blocking that they could cause, it could negate much of the benefit inherent in the vastly increased speed of in-memory processing. Instead, SQL Server In-Memory OLTP delivers a completely lock- and latch-free system, and true optimistic multi-version concurrency control (Chapter 5).

Other potential bottlenecks were the existing CHECKPOINT and transaction logging processes. The need to write to durable storage still exists for in-memory tables, but in SQL Server In-Memory OLTP these processes are adapted to be much more efficient, in order to prevent them becoming performance limiting, especially given the potential to support vastly increased workloads (Chapter 6).

The final bottleneck derives from the fact that the SQL Server query processor is essentially an interpreter; it re-processes statements continually, at runtime. It is not a true compiler. Of course, this is not a major performance concern, when the cost of physically reading data pages into memory from disk dwarfs the cost of query interpretation. However, once there is no cost of reading pages, the difference in efficiency between interpreting queries and running compiled queries can be enormous. Consequently, the new SQL Server In-Memory OLTP engine component provides the ability to create natively compiled procedures, i.e. machine code, for our most commonly executed data processing operations (Chapter 7).

Finally, we turn our attention to tools for managing SQL Server In-Memory OLTP structures, for monitoring and tuning performance, and finally, considerations for migrating existing OLTP workloads over to in-memory (Chapter 8).

Intended Audience and Prerequisites

This book is for anyone using SQL Server as a programmer or as an administrator who wants to understand how the new Hekaton engine works behind the scenes. It is specifically a book about Hekaton *internals*, focusing on details of memory-optimized tables and indexes, how the in-memory engine delivers transactional consistency (ACID compliance) without locking or latching, and the mechanics of its checkpointing, logging and garbage collection mechanisms.

SQL Server In-Memory OLTP is a new technology and this is not a book specifically on performance tuning and best practices. However, as you learn about how the Hekaton engine works internally to process your queries, certain best practices and opportunities for performance tuning will become obvious.

This book does not assume that you're a SQL Server expert, but I do expect that you have basic technical competency and familiarity with the standard SQL Server engine, and relative fluency with basic SQL statements.

You should have access to a SQL Server 2014 installation, even if it is the Evaluation edition, available free from Microsoft:
HTTP://TECHNET.MICROSOFT.COM/EN-GB/EVALCENTER/DN205290.ASPX.

The Hands-On Exercises

This book will provide the reader with scripts for hands-on exercises, shown as listings, to create memory-optimized databases, tables and indexes and to explore some aspects of Hekaton behavior. My examples were all created using SQL Server Management Studio (SSMS), and formatted automatically using Red Gate's SQL Prompt tool (the latter is an optional tool).

You can download these scripts from the following URL:
WWW.SIMPLE-TALK.COM/RedGateBooks/KalenDelaney/SQLServerHekaton_Code.zip.

All examples have been verified on SQL Server 2014 RTM (12.0.2000.8). All of the examples use custom-built example databases, as defined in the text.

Chapter 1: What's Special About In-Memory OLTP?

SQL Server 2014's In-Memory OLTP feature provides a suite of technologies for working with **memory-optimized** tables, in addition to the **disk-based tables** which SQL Server has always provided.

The SQL Server team designed the in-memory OLTP engine to be transparently accessible through familiar interfaces such as T-SQL and SQL Server Management Studio (SSMS). Therefore, during most data processing operations, users may be unaware that they are working with memory-optimized tables rather than disk-based ones.

However, SQL Server works with the data very differently if it is stored in memory-optimized tables. This chapter describes, at a high level, some of the fundamental differences between data storage structures and data operations, when working with memory-optimized, rather than standard disk-based tables and indexes.

It will also discuss SQL Server In-Memory OLTP in the context of similar, competing memory-optimized database solutions, and explain why the former is different.

Isn't In-Memory OLTP Just an Improved DBCC PINTABLE?

Let's dispel this myth right at the start: SQL Server In-Memory OLTP bears no relation or similarities at all to `DBCC PINTABLE`, a feature available in older versions of SQL Server that would not remove any data pages from a "pinned" table from memory, once those pages were read from disk.

These pinned tables were no different than any other disk-based tables. They required the same amount of locking, latching and logging and they used the same index structures, which also required locking and logging.

By contrast, as we'll discuss through this and subsequent chapters, the memory-optimized tables in SQL Server In-Memory OLTP are completely different than SQL Server disk-based tables. They use different data and index structures, and SQL Server takes no locks or latches on these structures during reading or writing, so it can allow concurrent access without blocking. Also, logging changes to memory-optimized tables is usually much more efficient than logging changes to disk-based tables.

The New In-Memory OLTP Component

In-memory OLTP is integrated with the SQL Server relational engine, allowing us to access in-memory data using standard interfaces such as T-SQL and SSMS, transparently. However, its internal behavior and capabilities are very different than those of the standard relational engine. In addition, in-memory OLTP allows an entirely new, highly efficient access path, using natively compiled stored procedures.

Figure 1-1 gives an overview of the SQL Server engine with the in-memory OLTP components. On the left side, we have the **memory optimized tables and indexes**, added as part of in-memory OLTP and, on the right we see the disk-based tables, which use the data structures that SQL Server has always used, and which require writing and reading 8 K data pages, as a unit, to and from disk.

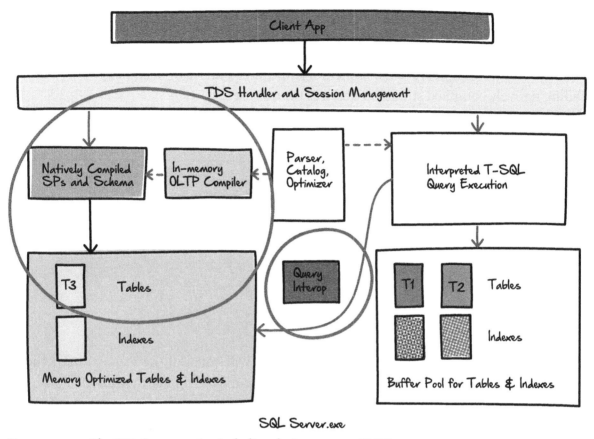

Figure 1-1: The SQL Server engine including the in-memory OLTP components.

In-memory OLTP also supports **natively compiled stored procedures**, an object type that is compiled to machine code by a new in-memory OLTP compiler and which has the potential to offer a further performance boost beyond that available solely from the use of memory-optimized tables. The standard counterpart is **interpreted T-SQL** stored procedures, which is what SQL Server has always used. Natively compiled stored procedures can reference only memory-optimized tables.

The **Query Interop** component allows interpreted T-SQL to reference memory-optimized tables. If a transaction can reference both memory-optimized tables and disk-based tables, we refer to it as a **cross-container** transaction.

19

Notice that the client application uses the same TDS Handler (Tabular Data Stream, the underlying networking protocol that is used to communicate with SQL Server), regardless of whether it is accessing memory-optimized tables or disk-based tables, or calling natively compiled stored procedures or interpreted T-SQL.

Memory-optimized tables

This section takes a broad look at three of the key differences between memory-optimized tables and their disk-based counterparts; subsequent chapters will fill in the details.

Entirely in-memory storage

When accessing disk-based tables, the data we need will hopefully be resident in memory, although it may not be. If not, the engine needs to read from disk the required data pages. This basic assumption that the data pages reside on disk underpins all data operations against disk-based tables, with user processes acquiring locks to protect data pages, in the buffer cache, from the effects of concurrent transactions, and SQL Server acquiring latches on pages as it reads them from, and writes them to, disk.

The first and perhaps most fundamental difference when using memory-optimized tables is that the **whole table and its indexes are stored in memory** all the time. Therefore, when accessing in-memory data structures, user processes will always find the required data in-memory. Concurrent data operations require no locking or latching whatsoever, thanks to a new, truly optimistic concurrency model, which we'll get to shortly.

As user processes modify in-memory data, SQL Server still needs to perform some disk I/O for any table that we wish to be durable, in others words where we wish a table to retain the in-memory data in the event of a server crash or restart. We'll return to this a little later in this chapter, in the *Data durability and recovery* section.

Row-based storage structure

The second big difference between disk-based tables and memory-optimized tables is in their underlying storage structure. The former is optimized for *block-addressable* disk storage, whereas the latter is optimized for *byte-addressable* memory storage.

For disk-based tables, SQL Server organizes data rows into 8 K units called data pages, with space allocated from extents, on disk. The data page is the basic unit of storage on disk and in memory. When SQL Server reads and writes data from disk, it reads and writes the relevant data pages. A data page will only contain data from one table or index. User processes modify rows on various data pages as required, and later, during a CHECKPOINT process, SQL Server first hardens the log records to disk and then writes all dirty pages to disk, the latter operation often causing a lot of "random" physical I/O.

For memory-optimized tables, there are no data pages, and no extents; there are just "data rows," written to memory sequentially, in the order the transactions occurred, with each row containing an index "pointer" to the next row. All "I/O" is then in-memory scanning of these structures. It means there is no notion of data rows being written to a particular location that "belongs" to a specified object. However, this is *not* to imply that memory-optimized tables are stored as unorganized sets of data rows, like a disk-based heap. In fact, every CREATE TABLE statement for a memory-optimized table must also create at least one **index** that SQL Server can use to link together all the data rows for that table (see the later section on *Indexes on memory-optimized tables*).

Each data row consists of two areas, the **row header** and then the **payload**, which is the actual column data. We'll discuss this structure in much more detail in Chapter 3, but the information stored in the row header includes the identity of the statement that created the row, pointers for each index on the target table and, critically, some **timestamp** values. There will be a timestamp recording the time a transaction inserted a row, and another indicating the time a transaction deleted a row. SQL Server records updates by inserting a new version of the row and marking the old version as "deleted." The actual cleanup of row versions that are no longer required, which involves unlinking them from index structures and removing them from memory, is a cooperative process involving both users threads and a dedicated garbage collection thread (more on this in Chapter 5).

As this implies, many versions of the same row can coexist at any given time. This allows concurrent access of the same row, during data modifications, with SQL Server displaying the row version relevant to each transaction according to the time the transaction started relative to the timestamps of the row version. This is the essence of the new **multi-version concurrency control** (MVCC) mechanism for in-memory tables, which we'll describe in a little more detail later in the chapter.

Native compilation of tables

The final significant difference between disk-based and memory-optimized tables is that the latter are **natively compiled**. When we create a memory-optimized table or index, SQL Server describes the structure of each table and its indexes in the metadata for that table. It then uses this metadata to compile into a DLL a set of native language routines (from an intermediate, auto-generated C language step) just for accessing that table. These DLLs are associated with the database, but not actually part of it.

In other words, SQL Server holds in memory, not only the table and index structures, but also a set of DLLs for accessing and modifying these data structures. The table metadata encodes into each DLL a set of native language algorithms that describe precisely the row format for the table and how to traverse its indexes, thus providing highly efficient access paths for the table data. This explains why we cannot alter a table, once created; if the table were altered, SQL Server would have to regenerate all the DLLs for table operations.

These DLLs result in much faster data access than is possible via the traditional way of using interpreted metadata. A big success of the implementation of in-memory OLTP is to have made these operations "invisible" to the user.

Natively compiled stored procedures

The best execution performance is obtained when using natively compiled stored procedures to access memory-optimized tables, which are also natively compiled, as described above.

Natively compiled stored procedures consist of processor instructions that can be executed directly by the CPU, without the need for further compilation or interpretation. Also, a natively compiled procedure will generate far fewer CPU instructions for the engine to execute than the equivalent interpreted T-SQL stored procedure.

However, there are limitations on the T-SQL language constructs that are allowed inside a natively compiled stored procedure, compared to the rich feature set available with interpreted code. In addition, natively compiled stored procedures can only access memory-optimized tables and cannot reference disk-based tables. Chapter 7 discusses natively compiled stored procedures in detail.

Concurrency improvements: the new MVCC model

SQL Server's traditional pessimistic concurrency control mechanisms, when accessing disk-based tables, use locks and latches to prevent "interference" between concurrent transactions on the same data rows, and so preserve the ACID characteristics of each transaction. Readers take shared locks on a resource to prevent writers from modifying that data until the reading statement (or transaction, depending on the transaction isolation level) commits or rolls back. Writers take exclusive locks to prevent other readers and writers from accessing "in-transit" data. In other words, transactions often have to pause processing while they wait to acquire locks (or latches) on a resource.

SQL Server 2005 and later introduced a "sort of" optimistic version of concurrency control, using the snapshot-based isolation levels, and maintaining previous row versions in a `tempdb` version store. Under this model, readers no longer acquire shared locks.

Instead of blocking, when one transaction needs to read rows that another transaction is modifying, the reader retrieves, from the version store, the previously committed values of the set of rows it needs. Therefore, SQL Server can preserve the ACID properties without having readers block writers, and without writers blocking readers. However, SQL Server still acquires locks during data modifications and so writers still block other writers.

Traditional locking, latching and concurrency control

We won't discuss any further in this book the locking, latching or concurrency mechanisms for disk-based tables. For full details, please refer to my book, SQL Server Concurrency: Locking, Blocking and Row Versioning (HTTP://TINYURL.COM/Q2UYB9B).

In contrast, SQL Server In-Memory OLTP introduces a truly optimistic MVCC model. It uses row versioning but its implementation bears little relation to the snapshot-based model used for disk-based tables. When accessing memory-optimized tables and index structures, SQL Server still supports the ACID properties of transactions, but it does so without ever using locking or latching to provide transaction isolation. This means that no transaction ever has, for lock-related reasons, to wait to read or modify a data row. Readers never block writers, writers never block readers, and writers never block writers.

Waits on memory-optimized tables

Transactions never acquire locks on memory-optimized tables, so they never have to wait to acquire them. However, this does not mean there is never any waiting when working with memory-optimized tables in a multi-user system. However, the waiting that does occur is usually of very short duration, such as when SQL Server is waiting for dependencies to be resolved during the validation phase of transaction processing (more on the validation phase in Chapters 3 and 5). Transactions might also need to wait for log writes to complete although, since the logging required when making changes to memory-optimized tables is much more efficient than logging for disk-based tables, the wait times will be much shorter.

No locks

Operations on disk-based tables implement the requested level of transaction isolation by using locks to make sure that a transaction (Tx2) cannot change data that another transaction (Tx1) needs to remain unchanged.

In a traditional relational database system, in which SQL Server needs to read pages from disk before it can process them, the cost of acquiring and managing locks can be just a fraction of the total wait time. Often, this cost is dwarfed by the overhead of waiting for disk reads, and managing the pages in the buffer pool.

However, if SQL Server were to acquire locks on memory-optimized tables, then locking waits would likely become the major overhead, since there is no cost at all for reading pages from disk.

Instead, the team designed SQL Server In-Memory OLTP to be a totally lock-free system. Fundamentally, this is possible because SQL Server never modifies any existing row, and so there is no need to lock them. Instead, an **UPDATE** operation creates a new version by marking the previous version of the row as deleted, and then inserting a new version of the row with new values. If a row is updated multiple times, there may be many versions of the same row existing simultaneously. SQL Server presents the correct version of the row to the requesting transaction by examining timestamps stored in the row header and comparing them to the transaction start time.

No latches

Latches are lightweight synchronization mechanisms (often called primitives as they are the smallest possible synchronization device), used by the SQL Server engine to guarantee consistency of the data structures that underpin disk-based tables, including index and data pages as well as internal structures such as non-leaf pages in a B-tree. Even though latches are quite a bit lighter weight than locks, there can still be substantial overhead and wait time involved in using latches.

When accessing disk-based tables, SQL Server must acquire a latch every time it reads a page from disk, to make sure no other transaction writes to the page while it is being read. It acquires a latch on the memory buffer into which it will read the page, to make sure no other transaction uses that buffer. In addition, SQL Server acquires latches on internal metadata, such as the internal table that keeps track of locks being acquired and released.

One key improvement provided by SQL Server In-Memory OLTP is that there is no page construct for memory-optimized tables. There is a page structure used for range indexes, but the way the pages are managed is completely different than the way they are managed for disk-based tables in a traditional database system. Not having to manage pages fundamentally changes the data operation algorithms from being disk optimized to being memory and cache optimized.

SQL Server In-Memory OLTP doesn't do any reading from disk during data processing, doesn't store data in buffers and doesn't apply any locks, and there is no reason for it to acquire latches for operations on memory-optimized tables, and therefore this eliminates one more possible source of waiting.

Indexes on memory-optimized tables

Indexes perform the same purpose for memory-optimized tables as their disk-based counterparts. However, again, under the covers they are very different structures.

With disk-based storage structures, there are data pages that combine sets of rows into a single structure. With in-memory structures, there are no such pages and instead SQL Server uses indexes to combine all the rows that belong to a table into a single structure. This is why every memory-optimized table must have at least one index.

We create indexes as part of table creation; unlike for disk-based indexes, we cannot use `CREATE INDEX` to create memory-optimized indexes. If we create a `PRIMARY KEY` on a column, and durable memory-optimized tables must have a `PRIMARY KEY`, then

SQL Server automatically creates a unique index on that column (and that it is the only allowed unique index). We can create a maximum of eight indexes on a memory-optimized table, including the PRIMARY KEY index.

Like tables, SQL Server stores memory-optimized indexes entirely in memory. However, unlike for tables, SQL Server never logs operations on indexes, and never persists indexes to the on-disk checkpoint files (covered shortly). SQL Server maintains indexes automatically during all modification operations on memory-optimized tables, just like B-tree indexes on disk-based tables, but in case of a restart, SQL Server rebuilds the indexes on the memory-optimized tables as the data is streamed into memory.

Memory-optimized tables support two basic types of index, both of which are non-clustered structures: **hash indexes** and **range indexes**.

A **hash index** is a new type of SQL Server index, specifically for memory-optimized tables, which are useful for performing lookups on specific values. A hash index, which is stored as a hash table, is essentially an array of hash buckets, where each bucket points to the location in memory of a data row. SQL Server applies a hash function to the index key values, and maps each one to the appropriate bucket. In each bucket is a pointer to a single row, the first row in the list of rows that hash to the same value. From that row, all other rows in the hash bucket are joined in a singularly linked-list (this will become clearer when we get to see some diagrams in Chapter 4).

A non-clustered **range index**, useful for retrieving ranges of values, is more like the sort of index we're familiar with when working with disk-based tables. However, again, the structure is different. The memory-optimized counterparts use a special **Bw-tree** storage structure.

A Bw-tree is similar to a disk-based B-tree index in that it has index pages organized into a root page, a leaf level, and possibly intermediate-level pages. However, the pages of a Bw-tree are very different structures from their disk-based counterparts. The pages can be of varying sizes, and the pages themselves are never modified; new pages are created when necessary, when the underlying rows are modified.

Data durability and recovery

For memory-optimized data structures, both tables and indexes, all the data is stored in memory, all the time. However, in order to continue to ensure the durability of the data, assuming that's required, SQL Server logs operations on memory-optimized tables (not indexes) to the same transaction log that is used to log operations on disk-based tables and, as always, the transaction log is stored on disk.

Efficient logging for in-memory data

We'll discuss this topic in much more detail in Chapter 6, but logging for in-memory tables is more efficient than for disk-based tables essentially because, given the same workload, SQL Server will write far fewer log records for an in-memory table than for its equivalent disk-based table. For example, it doesn't log any changes to data in indexes. It will also never write log records associated with uncommitted transactions, since SQL Server will never write dirty data to disk for in-memory tables. Also, rather than write every atomic change as a single log record, in-memory OLTP will combine many changes into a single log record.

SQL Server In-Memory OLTP also continuously persists the table data to disk in special **checkpoint** files. It uses these files *only* for database recovery, and only ever writes to them "offline," using a background thread. Therefore, when we create a database that will use memory-optimized data structures, we must create, not only the data file (used only for disk-based table storage) and the log file, but also a special MEMORY_OPTIMIZED_ DATA filegroup that will contain the checkpoint file pairs, each pair consisting of a **data** checkpoint file and a **delta** checkpoint file (more on these in Chapter 2).

These checkpoint files are append-only and SQL Server writes to them strictly sequentially, in the order of the transactions in the transaction log, to minimize the I/O cost. In case of a system crash or server shutdown, SQL Server can recreate the rows of data in the memory-optimized tables from the checkpoint files and the transaction log.

When we insert a data row into a memory-optimized table, the background thread (called the offline checkpoint thread) will, at some point, append the inserted row to the corresponding data checkpoint file. Likewise, when we delete a row, the thread will append a reference to the deleted row to the corresponding delta checkpoint file. So, a "deleted" row remains in the data file but the corresponding delta file records the fact that it was deleted. As the checkpoint files grow, SQL Server will at some point merge them, so that rows marked as deleted actually get deleted from the data checkpoint file, and create a new file pair. Again, further details of how all this works come in Chapter 6.

In-memory OLTP does provide the option to create a table that is non-durable, using an option called SCHEMA_ONLY. As the option indicates, SQL Server will log the table creation, so the table schema will be durable, but will not log any data manipulation language (DML) on the table, so the data will not be durable. These tables do not require any I/O operations during transaction processing, but the data is only available in memory while SQL Server is running. These non-durable tables could be useful in certain cases, for example as staging tables in ETL scenarios or for storing web server session state.

In the event of a SQL Server shutdown, or an AlwaysOn Availability Group failover, the data in these tables is lost. When SQL Server runs recovery on the database, it will recreate the tables but without the data. Although the data is not durable, operations on these tables meet all the other transactional requirements; they are atomic, isolated, and consistent.

We'll see how to create both durable and non-durable tables in Chapter 2.

SQL Server In-Memory OLTP in Context

SQL Server In-Memory OTLP is far from the only product to offer optimized in-memory storage and processing of OLTP data. Let's round off the chapter with a brief review of competitive offerings.

For processing OLTP data, there are two types of specialized engines. The first type are main-memory databases. Oracle has TimesTen, IBM has SolidDB and there are many others that primarily target the embedded database space. The second type are applications caches or key-value stores (for example, Velocity / App Fabric Cache and Gigaspaces) that leverage application and middle-tier memory to offload work from the database system. These caches continue to become more sophisticated and acquire database capabilities, such as transactions, range indexing, and query capabilities (Gigaspaces already has these, for example). At the same time, database systems are acquiring cache capabilities like high-performance hash indexes and scale across a cluster of machines (VoltDB is an example).

The in-memory OLTP engine is meant to offer the best of both of these types of engines, providing all of the afore-mentioned features. One way to think of in-memory OLTP is that it has the performance of a cache and the capability of a database. It supports storing your tables and indexes in memory, so you can create an entire database to be a complete in-memory system. It also offers high-performance indexes and logging as well as other features to significantly improve query execution performance.

SQL Server In-Memory OLTP offers the following features that few or any of the competition's products provide:

- no storage of data on pages, removing the need for page latches
- hash and Bw-tree indexes specifically optimized for main-memory access
- true multi-version optimistic concurrency control with no locking or latching for any operations

- natively compiled stored procedures to improve execution time for basic data manipulation operations by orders of magnitude

- integration between memory-optimized tables and disk-based tables so that the transition to a memory resident database can be made gradually, creating only your most critical tables and stored procedures as memory-optimized objects.

Unlike in-memory OLTP, a lot of its competitors still use traditional page constructs, even while the pages are forced to stay in memory. For example SAP HANA still uses 16 KB pages for its in-memory row-store, which would inherently suffer from page latch contention in a high-performance environment.

The most notable difference in design of SQL Server In-Memory OLTP from competitors' products is the "interop" integration. In a typical high-end OLTP workload, the performance bottlenecks are concentrated in specific areas, such as a small set of tables and stored procedures. It would be costly and inefficient to force the whole database to be resident in memory. But, to date, the other main competitive products require such an approach. In SQL Server's case, the high performance and high contention area can be migrated to in-memory OLTP, then the operations (stored procedures) on those memory-optimized tables can be natively compiled to achieve maximum business processing performance.

This "interop" capability is possible because SQL Server In-Memory OLTP is fully integrated in the SQL Server database engine, meaning you can use the same familiar APIs, language, development, and administration tools; and, most importantly, you can exploit the knowledge your organization has built up using SQL Server to also work with in-memory OLTP. Some competitor products can act like a cache for relational data, but are not integrated. Other products provide support only for in-memory tables, and any disk-based tables must be managed through a traditional relational database.

Summary

This first chapter took a first, broad-brush look at the new SQL Server In-Memory OLTP engine. Memory-optimized data structures are entirely resident in memory, so user processes will always find the data they need by traversing these structures in memory, without the need for disk I/O. Furthermore, the new MVCC model means that SQL Server can mediate concurrent access of these data structures, and ensure ACID transaction properties, without the use of any locks and latches; no user transactions against memory-optimized data structures will ever be forced to wait to acquire a lock!

Natively compiled stored procedures provide highly efficient data access to these data structures, offering a further performance boost. Even the logging mechanisms for memory-optimized tables, to ensure transaction durability, are far more efficient than for standard disk-based tables.

Combined, all these features make the use of SQL Server In-Memory OLTP a very attractive proposition for many OLTP workloads. Of course, as ever, it is no silver bullet. While it can and will offer substantial performance improvements to many applications, its use requires careful planning, and almost certainly some redesign of existing tables and procedures, as we'll discuss as we progress deeper into this book.

Additional Resources

As with any "v1" release of a new technology, the pace of change is likely to be rapid. We plan to revise this book to reflect significant advances in subsequent releases, but in the meantime it's likely that new online information about in-memory OLTP will appear with increasing frequency.

As well as bookmarking the online documentation for in-memory OLTP (see below), you should keep your eyes on whatever Microsoft has to say on the topic, on their SQL Server website (HTTP://WWW.MICROSOFT.COM/SQLSERVER), on the TechNet TechCenter (HTTP://TECHNET.MICROSOFT.COM/EN-US/SQLSERVER/) and on the MSDN DevCenter (HTTP://MSDN.MICROSOFT.COM/EN-US/SQLSERVER).

- **SQL Server 2014 online documentation** – high-level information about SQL Server's In-Memory OLTP:

  HTTP://TINYURL.COM/NBCEYZ9.

- **Wikipedia** – general background about in-memory databases, with links to other vendors:

  HTTP://EN.WIKIPEDIA.ORG/WIKI/IN-MEMORY_DATABASE.

- **Hekaton: SQL Server's Memory-Optimized OLTP Engine** – a publication submitted to the ACM by the team at Microsoft Research that was responsible for the Hekaton project:

  HTTP://TINYURL.COM/LCL26XS.

- **The Path to In-Memory Database Technology** – an excellent blog post about the history of relational databases and the path that led to in-memory OLTP:

  HTTP://TINYURL.COM/N9YV6RP.

Chapter 2: Creating and Accessing In-Memory OLTP Databases and Tables

In-memory OLTP is an automatic and obligatory component of the SQL Server setup process for any installation of a 64-bit Enterprise or Developer edition of SQL Server 2014 that includes the database engine components. In-memory OLTP is not available at all with 32-bit editions.

Therefore, with no further setup, we can begin creating databases and data structures that will store memory-optimized data.

Creating Databases

Any database that will contain memory-optimized tables needs to have a single MEMORY_OPTIMIZED_DATA filegroup containing at least one container, which stores the checkpoint files needed by SQL Server to recover the memory-optimized tables. These are the checkpoint data and delta files that we introduced briefly in Chapter 1. SQL Server populates these files during CHECKPOINT operations, and reads them during the recovery process, which we'll discuss in Chapter 6.

The syntax for creating a MEMORY_OPTIMIZED_DATA filegroup is almost the same as that for creating a regular FILESTREAM filegroup, but it must specify the option CONTAINS MEMORY_OPTIMIZED_DATA. Listing 2-1 provides an example of a CREATE DATABASE statement for a database that can support memory-optimized tables (edit the path names to match your system; if you create the containers on the same drive you'll need to differentiate the two file names).

```
USE master
GO
IF EXISTS (SELECT * FROM sys.databases WHERE name='HKDB')
     DROP DATABASE HKDB;
GO
  CREATE DATABASE HKDB
    ON
    PRIMARY(NAME = [HKDB_data],
         FILENAME = 'Q:\DataHK\HKDB_data.mdf', size=500MB),
    FILEGROUP [HKDB_mod_fg] CONTAINS MEMORY_OPTIMIZED_DATA
         (NAME = [HKDB_mod_dir],
          FILENAME = 'R:\DataHK\HKDB_mod_dir'),
         (NAME = [HKDB_mod_dir],
          FILENAME = 'S:\DataHK\HKDB_mod_dir')

    LOG ON (name = [HKDB_log],
            Filename='L:\LogHK\HKDB_log.ldf', size=500MB)
    COLLATE Latin1_General_100_BIN2;
```

Listing 2-1:   Creating a database.

In Listing 2-1, we create a regular data file (`HKDB_data.mdf`), used for disk-based table storage only, and a regular log file (`HKDB_log.ldf`). In addition, we create a memory-optimized filegroup, `HKDB_mod_fg` with, in this case, two file containers each called `HKDB_mod_dir`. These containers host data and delta checkpoint file pairs to which the `CHECKPOINT` process will write data, for use during database recovery. The data checkpoint file stores inserted rows and the delta files reference deleted rows. The data and delta file for each pair may be in the same or different containers, depending on the number of containers specified. In this case, with two containers, one will contain the data checkpoint files and the other the delta checkpoint files, for each pair. If we had only one container, it would contain both the data and delta files.

Notice that we place the primary data file, each of the checkpoint file containers, and the transaction log, on separate drives. Even though the data in a memory-optimized table is never read from or written to disk "inline" during query processing, it can still be useful to consider placement of your checkpoint files and log file for optimum I/O performance during logging, checkpoint, and recovery.

To help ensure optimum recovery speed, you will want to put each of the containers in the `MEMORY_OPTIMIZED` filegroup on a separate drive, with fast sequential I/O.

To reduce any log waits, and improve overall transaction throughput, it's best to place the log file on a drive with fast random I/O, such as an SSD drive. As the use of memory-optimized tables allows for a much greater throughput, we'll start to see a lot of activity needing to be written to the transaction log although, as we'll see in Chapter 6, the overall efficiency of the logging process is much higher for in-memory tables than for disk-based tables.

Finally, notice that Listing 2-1 specifies a **binary collation**. In the current version of in-memory OLTP, any indexes on character columns in memory-optimized tables can only be on columns that use a Windows (non-SQL) `BIN2` collation, and natively compiled procedures only support comparisons, sorting and grouping on those same collations. In this listing, we use the `CREATE DATABASE` command to define a default binary collation for the entire database, which means that this collation will apply to object names (i.e. the metadata) as well as user data, and so all table names will be case sensitive. An object called `SalesOrders` will not be recognized if a query uses `salesorders`. As such, unless every table in a database will be a memory-optimized table, it is better to specify the collation for each of the character columns in any memory-optimized table. We can also specify the collation in the query, for use in any comparison, sorting or grouping operation.

If, instead of creating a new database, we want to allow an existing database to store memory-optimized objects and data, we simply add a `MEMORY_OPTIMIZED_DATA` filegroup to an existing database, and then add a container to that filegroup, as shown in Listing 2-2.

```
ALTER DATABASE MyAW2012
     ADD FILEGROUP MyAW2012_mod_fg CONTAINS MEMORY_OPTIMIZED_DATA;
GO
ALTER DATABASE MyAW2012
     ADD FILE (NAME='MyAW012_mod_dir',
                  FILENAME='c:\DataHK\MyAW2012_mod_dir')
      TO FILEGROUP MyAW2012_mod_fg;
GO
```

Listing 2-2:   Adding a filegroup and file for storing memory-optimized table data.

Creating Tables

The syntax for creating memory-optimized tables is almost identical to the syntax for creating disk-based tables, but with a few required extensions, and a few restrictions on the data types, indexes, constraints and other options, that memory-optimize tables can support.

To specify that a table is a memory-optimized table, we use the MEMORY_OPTIMIZED = ON clause. Apart from that, and assuming we're using only the *supported* data types and other objects, the only other requirement is that we include at least one index, as part of the CREATE TABLE statement. Listing 2-3 shows a basic example.

```
USE HKDB;
GO

CREATE TABLE T1
(
   [Name] varchar(32) not null PRIMARY KEY NONCLUSTERED HASH
                                   WITH (BUCKET_COUNT = 100000),
   [City] varchar(32) null,
   [State_Province] varchar(32) null,
   [LastModified] datetime not null,

) WITH (MEMORY_OPTIMIZED = ON, DURABILITY = SCHEMA_AND_DATA);
```

Listing 2-3:   Creating a memory-optimized table with the index definition inline.

The following sections will examine each element of creating memory-optimized tables, covering durability, defining indexes and constraints, and finally data type and other restrictions.

Durability

We can define a memory-optimized table with one of two DURABILITY values: SCHEMA_ AND_DATA or SCHEMA_ONLY, with the former being the default. If we define a memory-optimized table with DURABILITY=SCHEMA_ONLY, then SQL Server will not log changes to the table's data, nor will it persist the data in the table to the checkpoint files, on disk. However, it will still persist the schema (i.e. the table structure) as part of the database metadata, so the empty table will be available after the database is recovered during a SQL Server restart.

Indexes and constraints

We can create up to a total of eight non-clustered indexes on a memory-optimized table (clustered indexes are not supported). These non-clustered indexes can include **range indexes**, the default if we don't specify an index type, and **hash indexes**.

As discussed in Chapter 1, every memory-optimized table must have at least one index, to join together the rows that belong to that table. We can satisfy this "at least one index" requirement for in-memory tables by specifying a PRIMARY KEY constraint, since SQL Server automatically creates an index to support this constraint. We must declare a PRIMARY KEY on all tables except for those created with the SCHEMA_ONLY option.

In the previous example (Listing 2-3), we declared a PRIMARY KEY constraint on the Name column, and specified the type of index that should be created to support the constraint, in this case, a HASH index. When we create a hash index, we must also specify a bucket count (i.e. the number of buckets in the hash index).

We'll cover hash indexes in Chapter 4, where we'll also discuss a few guidelines for choosing a value for the BUCKET_COUNT attribute.

We can create any type of single-column index, hash or range, inline with the column definition. For example, we might, alternatively, have specified a range index for the PRIMARY KEY column and a hash index on the City column, as shown in Listing 2-4.

```
CREATE TABLE T1
(
    [Name] varchar(32) not null PRIMARY KEY NONCLUSTERED
                                   WITH (BUCKET_COUNT = 100000),
    [City] varchar(32) not null INDEX T1_hdx_c2 HASH
                           WITH (BUCKET_COUNT = 10000),
    [State_Province] varchar(32) null,
    [LastModified] datetime not null,

) WITH (MEMORY_OPTIMIZED = ON, DURABILITY = SCHEMA_AND_DATA);
```

Listing 2-4:   Creating an in-memory table with 2 indexes defined inline.

For non-PRIMARY KEY columns the NONCLUSTERED keyword is optional, but we have to specify it explicitly when defining the PRIMARY KEY because otherwise SQL Server will try to create a clustered index, the default for a PRIMARY KEY, and will generate an error because clustered indexes are not allowed on memory-optimized tables.

For composite indexes, we create them after the column definitions. Listing 2-5 creates a new table, T2, with the same hash index for the primary key on the Name column, plus a range index on the City and State_Province columns.

If you're wondering why we created a new table, T2, rather than just adding the composite index to the existing T1, it's because the SQL Server stores the structure of in-memory tables as part of the database metadata, and so we can't alter those tables once created.

```
CREATE TABLE T2
(
    [Name] varchar(32) not null PRIMARY KEY NONCLUSTERED HASH
                                WITH (BUCKET_COUNT = 100000),
    [City] varchar(32) not null,
    [State_Province] varchar(32) not null,
    [LastModified] datetime not null,

  INDEX T1_ndx_c2c3 NONCLUSTERED ([City],[State_Province])

) WITH (MEMORY_OPTIMIZED = ON, DURABILITY = SCHEMA_AND_DATA);
```

Listing 2-5: Creating a memory-optimized table with the index definition specified separately.

In short, no schema changes are allowed once a table is created so, instead of using ALTER TABLE, we must drop and recreate the table. Likewise, we cannot use procedure sp_rename with memory-optimized tables, to change either the table name or any column names.

Also note that there are no specific index DDL commands (i.e. CREATE INDEX, ALTER INDEX, DROP INDEX). We always define indexes as part of the table creation.

There are a few other restrictions and limitations around the use of indexes, constraints and other properties, during table creation, as follows:

- no FOREIGN KEY or CHECK constraints

- IDENTITY columns can only be defined with SEED and INCREMENT of 1

- no UNIQUE indexes other than for the PRIMARY KEY

- a maximum of 8 indexes, including the index supporting the PRIMARY KEY.

Also note that we can't create DML triggers on a memory-optimized table.

Data type restrictions

A memory-optimized table can only have columns of these supported data types:

- `bit`

- all integer types: `tinyint`, `smallint`, `int`, `bigint`

- all money types: `money`, `smallmoney`

- all floating types: `float`, `real`

- date/time types: `datetime`, `smalldatetime`, `datetime2`, `date`, `time`

- numeric and decimal types

- all non-LOB string types: `char(n)`, `varchar(n)`, `nchar(n)`, `nvarchar(n)`, `sysname`

- non-LOB binary types: `binary(n)`, `varbinary(n)`

- `Uniqueidentifier`.

None of the LOB data types are allowed; there can be no columns of type `XML`, CLR or the max data types, and all row lengths are limited to 8060 bytes with no off-row data. In fact, the 8060 byte limit is enforced at table creation time, so unlike a disk-based table, a memory-optimized table with two `varchar(5000)` columns could not be created.

In addition, even though most of the same data types that are allowed for disk-based tables are also available for memory-optimized tables, in some cases the internal storage size may be different. The main differences are for those data types that allow varying precision values to be specified, as listed below.

- **Numeric/decimal**

  - In a disk-based table, storage size can be 5, 9, 13 or 17 bytes, depending on the precision.

  - In a memory-optimized table, storage size is either 8 or 16 bytes, depending on the precision.

- **Time**

  - In a disk-based table, storage size can be 3, 4 or 5 bytes, depending on the precision of the fractional seconds.

  - In a memory-optimized table, the time data type is always stored in 8 bytes.

- **Date**

  - In a disk-based table, storage is always 3 bytes.

  - In a memory-optimized table, storage is always 4 bytes.

- **Datetime2**

  - In a disk-based table, storage size can be 6, 7 or 8 bytes, depending on the precision of the fractional seconds (this is 3 bytes for the date, plus the bytes needed for time).

  - In a memory-optimized table, the `datetime2` data type is always stored in 8 bytes.

Accessing Memory-Optimized Tables with T-SQL

We can access memory-optimized tables in two different ways, either using interpreted T-SQL, via the Query Interop (see Chapter 1), or through T-SQL in natively compiled stored procedures.

The binary collation issue

As noted earlier, any column in a memory-optimized table that has a character data type and will participate in an index must use a `BIN2` collation, which uses an algorithm for sorting, grouping and comparison that is based on Unicode, and so is case sensitive.

In Listing 2-1, we created the `HKDB` database with a binary (`BIN2`) collation, so every table and column in the database will use this `BIN2` collation, so the data, including the metadata, is case sensitive.

Listing 2-6 shows a few simple examples of working with memory-optimized tables.

```
USE HKDB2;
GO
-- This statement will generate an error,
-- due to the case sensitivity of object names
SELECT  *
FROM    t1;
GO


-- This statement will succeed
SELECT  *
FROM    T1;
GO


-- Now insert three rows into the table
INSERT INTO T1 VALUES ('da Vinci','Vinci','FL',getdate());
INSERT INTO T1 VALUES ('Botticelli','Florence','FL',getdate());
INSERT INTO T1 VALUES ('Donatello','Florence','FL',getdate());
GO


-- The first SELECT returns no rows, the second fails because
-- of an invalid column name, the third succeeds
SELECT * FROM T1 WHERE Name = 'Da Vinci';
SELECT * FROM T1 WHERE name = 'da Vinci';
SELECT * FROM T1 WHERE Name = 'da Vinci';
GO


-- "da Vinci" appears last in the ordering because, with a
-- BIN2 collation, any upper-case characters sort before all
-- lower-case characters
SELECT * FROM T1 ORDER BY Name;


-- Set the collation in the query, to match instance collation
-- to return 'expected' results
SELECT * FROM T1 WHERE Name = 'Da Vinci' COLLATE Latin1_General_CI_AS;
SELECT * FROM T1 ORDER BY Name COLLATE Latin1_General_CI_AS;
```

Listing 2-6:   Querying tables in a database that uses a BIN2 collation.

The alternative, as discussed, is to create each character column in a given table with the BIN2 collation. For example, if we rerun Listing 2-1, but without specifying the collation then, when recreating table T1, we would specify the collation for each character column as part of the CREATE TABLE statement, and it would be obligatory to specify a BIN2 collation on the Name column, since this participates in the hash index.

```
USE HKDB;
GO
CREATE TABLE T1
(
    [Name] varchar(32) COLLATE Latin1_General_100_BIN2 not null
                                PRIMARY KEY NONCLUSTERED HASH
                                  WITH (BUCKET_COUNT = 100000),
    [City] varchar(32) COLLATE Latin1_General_100_BIN2 null,
    [State_Province]  varchar(32) COLLATE Latin1_General_100_BIN2 null,
    [LastModified] datetime not null,

) WITH (MEMORY_OPTIMIZED = ON, DURABILITY = SCHEMA_AND_DATA);
GO
```

Listing 2-7:   Specifying collations at the column level, during table creation.

Rerunning the queries in Listing 2-6, we'll see that this eliminates the case sensitivity on the table and column names, but the data case sensitivity remains.

Finally, remember that tempdb will use the collation for the SQL Server instance. If the instance does not use the same BIN2 collation, then any operations that use tempdb objects may encounter collation mismatch problems. One solution is to use COLLATE database_default for the columns on any temporary objects.

Interpreted T-SQL

When accessing memory-optimized tables using interpreted T-SQL, via the interop, we have access to virtually the full T-SQL surface area (i.e. the full list of statements and expressions). However, we should not expect the same performance as when we access memory-optimized tables using natively compiled stored procedures (Chapter 7 shows a performance comparison).

Use of interop is the appropriate choice when running ad hoc queries, or to use while migrating your applications to in-memory OLTP, as a step in the migration process, before migrating the most performance-critical procedures. Interpreted T-SQL should also be used when you need to access both memory-optimized tables and disk-based tables.

The only T-SQL features or capabilities not supported when accessing memory-optimized tables using interop are the following:

- TRUNCATE TABLE
- MERGE (when a memory-optimized table is the target)
- dynamic and keyset cursors (these are automatically degraded to static cursors)
- cross-database queries
- cross-database transactions
- accessing a memory-optimized table from a CLR module
- referencing a memory-optimized table in an index view
- linked servers
- locking hints: TABLOCK, XLOCK, PAGLOCK, etc. (NOLOCK is supported, but is quietly ignored)
- isolation level hints READUNCOMMITTED, READCOMMITTED and READCOMMITTEDLOCK.

T-SQL in natively compiled procedures

Natively compiled stored procedures offer the fastest way to execute T-SQL for access to data in memory-optimized tables. Note that we cannot access disk-based tables from within natively compiled stored procedures. Natively compiled procedures are targeted for OLTP applications, although that is certainly not a requirement. You will most likely find that you get the greatest performance improvement, compared to interop T-SQL, when your procedures are processing few rows with simple transactions, such as for an order entry table.

Currently, there are many more limitations on the T-SQL that we can use in these natively compiled procedures, as well as limitations on the data types and collations that natively compiled procedures can access and process. The MSDN documentation (see *Additional Resources*, below) provides a full list of supported and unsupported T-SQL statements, data types and operators. The reason for the restrictions is that, internally, a separate function must be created for each operation on each table. The interface will be expanded in subsequent versions.

However, there are also a few T-SQL features that are supported only in natively compiled stored procedures that are not available when using interpreted T-SQL code. These include:

- atomic blocks

- NOT NULL constraints on parameters and variables

- SCHEMABINDING.

Chapter 7 will describe these features, as well as providing details of how natively compiled stored procedures are processed.

Summary

This chapter covered the basics of creating database, tables and indexes to store memory-optimized data. In creating the database, we must define a special memory-optimized filegroup, which is built on the FILESTREAM technology. When creating a memory-optimized table, we just have to specify a special MEMORY_OPTIMIZED = ON clause, and create at least one index on the table. It sounds simple, and it is, but we have to remember that there are currently quite a number of restrictions on the data types, indexes, constraints, and other options, that memory-optimized tables can support. Also, any character column that participates in an index must use a BIN2 collation, which might affect the results of queries against this column.

We can access memory-optimized data structures with T-SQL, either in interop mode or via natively compiled stored procedures. In the former case, we can use more or less the full T-SQL surface area, but in the latter case, there is a longer list of restrictions.

Additional Resources

- **Details of supported query constructs in natively compiled procedures**:
  HTTP://TINYURL.COM/KX5JR5E.

- **Details of T-SQL Constructs Not Supported by In-Memory OLTP**:
  HTTP://TINYURL.COM/M7O4GD4.

- **White paper discussing SQL Server Filestream storage**, explaining how files in the filegroups containing memory-optimized data are organized and managed internally:
  HTTP://TINYURL.COM/O3ZRNP2.

Chapter 3: Row Structure and Multi-Version Concurrency

In the previous two chapters, we discussed how the storage structures for in-memory tables and indexes are very different from their disk-based counterparts. SQL Server does not store the data rows on pages, nor does it pre-allocate space for these pages from extents. Instead, it stores the data rows to memory, written sequentially in the order the transactions occurred, linked by pointers in an "index chain." SQL Server allocates space for rows in memory tables on the fly, from memory structures called heaps, which are different than the type of heaps SQL Server supports for disk-based tables.

SQL Server knows what rows belong to the same table because they are all connected using the tables' indexes. Each in-memory table must have at least one index, as this index provides structure for each table. An in-memory table can have up to eight indexes in total, comprising a mixture of both hash and range indexes (covered in Chapter 4), both of which are non-clustered structures.

The structure of a data row within a memory-optimized data structure reflects the fact that the in-memory OLTP engine supports a truly optimistic concurrency model, called a multi-version concurrency control (MVCC) model, which is based on in-memory **row versioning**. For memory-optimized tables, SQL Server never modifies any existing row. Instead, any UPDATE operation is a two-step process that marks the current version of the row as invalid and then creates a new version of the row. If a row is subject to multiple updates, then many versions of the same row will coexist simultaneously. SQL Server displays the correct version to each transaction that wishes to access a row by examining timestamps stored in the row header, and comparing them to the time the accessing transaction started.

In this chapter, we're going to explore the row structure that enables this row versioning, and then take a high-level view of how the new MVCC model works.

Row Structure

The data rows that comprise in-memory tables have a structure very different than the row structures used for disk-based tables. Each row consists of a **row header**, and a **payload** containing the row attributes (the actual data). Figure 3-1 shows this structure, as well as expanding on the content of the header area.

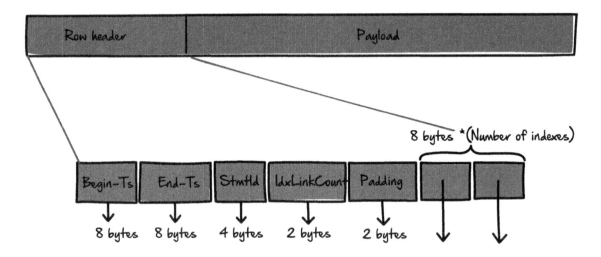

Figure 3-1:   The structure of a row in a memory-optimized table.

Row header

The row header for every data row consists of the following fields:

- **Begin-Ts** – the "insert" timestamp. It reflects the time that the transaction that inserted a row issued its COMMIT.

- **End-Ts** – the "delete" timestamp. It reflects the time that the transaction that deleted a row issued its COMMIT.

- **StmtId** – every statement within a transaction has a unique StmtId value, which identifies the statement that created the row. If the same row is then accessed again by the same statement, it can be ignored. This can provide Halloween protection within transactions on memory-optimized tables.

- **IdxLinkCount** – a reference count that indicates the number of indexes that reference this row.

- **Padding** – extra bytes added (and not used) so the row will be a multiple of 8 bytes in length.

- **Index Pointers** – these are C language pointers to the next row in the index chain. There is a pointer for each index on the table. It is the index pointers, plus the index data structures, that connect together the rows of a table. There are no other structures for combining rows into a table other than to link them together with the index pointers, which is why every table must have at least one index. We'll discuss this in more detail later in the chapter.

Payload area

The payload is the row data itself, containing the index key columns plus all the other columns in the row, meaning that all indexes on a memory-optimized table can be thought of as covering indexes. The payload format can vary depending on the table, and based on the table's schema. As described in Chapter 1, the in-memory OLTP compiler generates the DLLs for table operations. These DLLs contain code describing the payload format, and so can also generate the appropriate commands for all row operations.

Row Versions, Timestamps and the MVCC Model

As discussed briefly in Chapter 1, SQL Server In-Memory OLTP offers a truly optimistic MVCC system, enforcing ACID transaction properties, and the properties required by the transaction's isolation level (discussed in Chapter 5), without the need to acquire locks or latches, and so never requiring a command to wait for lock- or latch-related reasons.

Each time a transaction modifies a row, the in-memory engine creates a new version of the row. If a row is subject to multiple modifications, then multiple versions of the row will exist within memory, concurrently. Note that the storage engine really has no concept of "versions." It will simply "see" multiple rows using the index linkages and return each row that is valid, depending on the timestamp, and that meets the query's criteria. During query processing, the engine will determine which rows should be visible to the accessing transaction, by comparing the time the transaction started to the `Begin-Ts` and `End-Ts` timestamp values stored in the header of the row it is accessing.

Transaction IDs and timestamps

In order to support multiple row versions, every database that supports memory-optimized tables manages two internal counters:

- **The `Transaction-ID` counter** – this identifies each active transaction. It is a global, unique transaction id value (`xtp_transaction_id`) for the in-memory OLTP portion of a transaction. It is incremented every time a new transaction starts, and reset whenever the SQL Server instance restarts.

- **The Global Transaction Timestamp** – this is the "commit" timestamp. It is also a global and unique value, but not reset on a restart. SQL Server increments the value monotonically each time a transaction issues a COMMIT. From here in, I'll use the simple term *timestamp*, instead of Global Transaction Timestamp, to refer to this value.

SQL Server keeps track of each active transaction in an internal, global transaction table. When a transaction starts, SQL Server increments the `Transaction-ID` counter, and assigns a unique transaction ID to the transaction. When the transaction issues a `COMMIT`, SQL Server generates a commit timestamp, which it stores in the internal table initially, and then writes the value to the header of affected rows, once it validates the transaction and hardens the changes to the log.

SQL Server also stores in the internal table a system timestamp that indicates the transaction's start time; it is actually the timestamp for the last committed transaction at the time this transaction started and indicates when the transaction began, relative to the serialization order of the database. More than one transaction can have the same start timestamp. This start timestamp is never used anywhere else, and is only in the internal table while the transaction is active.

The commit timestamps of existing row versions and the start timestamps of the transaction determine which row versions each active transaction can see. The version of a row that an active transaction can see depends on the **validity interval** of the row version compared to the **logical read time** of the active transaction. Generally speaking the logical read time of the active transaction will be the time the transaction started, and we'll assume that here, but for the **READ COMMITTED** transaction isolation level (only available to auto-commit transactions – more on this in Chapter 5), it will be the time the actual statement executed. A transaction executing with logical read time **RT** must only see the effects of transactions with a start time of less than or equal to **RT**. It can see existing row versions with a commit timestamp for the `INSERT` (i.e. `Begin-Ts`) of less than or equal to RT, and a commit timestamp for the `DELETE` (i.e. `End-Ts`) of greater than RT.

For example, let's say an `INSERT` transaction issues a `COMMIT` at timestamp "5," inserting a new row with the value "white." At timestamp "10" an `UPDATE` to the same row commits, changing the value to "brown." Two versions of this row now coexist. At timestamp 10, the "white" version of the row is marked for deletion, with a commit timestamp of "10" for the delete, and the new "brown" row version is inserted, with a commit timestamp of "10" for the `INSERT`. We'll assume no subsequent transaction has touched the row.

In this example, the "white" version of the row has a validity interval of 5 to 10 and the "brown" row has a validity interval of 10 to infinity. An active transaction with a logical read time greater than or equal to 5, and less than 10, such as 5 or 9, should see the "white" row, whereas one that started at time 10 or higher should see the "brown" row version.

After a transaction issues a COMMIT, SQL Server performs some **validation checks** (more on this shortly). Having determined the transaction is valid, it hardens it to disk and writes the commit timestamp into the row header of all affected rows. If the transaction was an INSERT, it writes the commit timestamp to Begin-Ts and, if it was a DELETE, to End-Ts. An UPDATE is simply an atomic operation consisting of a DELETE followed by an INSERT.

Row versions and transaction processing phases

We'll discuss data operations and transaction processing in much more detail in Chapter 5, as well as the impact of transaction isolation levels. However, it's worth taking a preview here of a simple data modification example, examining how SQL Server creates various row versions, and what values it stores to the row headers at various phases of the processing. This will provide a good, high-level view of how the optimistic MVCC model works.

At the start of our example, we have two existing data rows. In the simplified depiction in Figure 3-2, the first column shows only the Begin-Ts and End-Ts value from the row header for each row, and the next two columns show the actual data values for the Name and City columns in the payload.

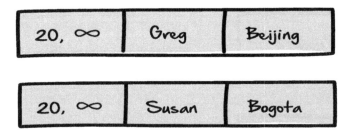

Figure 3-2:   Two rows, both inserted at timestamp 20.

We can see that a transaction inserted the rows <Greg, Beijing> and <Susan, Bogota> at timestamp 20. Notice that SQL Server uses a special value, referred to as "infinity," for the End-Ts value for rows that are active (not yet marked as invalid).

We're now going to assume that a user-defined transaction, with a Transaction-ID of Tx1, starts at timestamp 90 and will:

- delete <Susan, Bogota>

- update <Greg, Beijing> to <Greg, Lisbon>

- insert <Jane, Helsinki>.

Let's see how the row versions and their values evolve during the three basic stages (processing, validation, and post-processing) of this transaction, and how SQL Server controls which rows are visible to other active concurrent transactions.

Processing phase

During the processing stage, SQL Server processes the transaction, creating new row versions (and linking them into index structures – covered in Chapter 4), and marking rows for deletion as necessary, as shown in Figure 3-3.

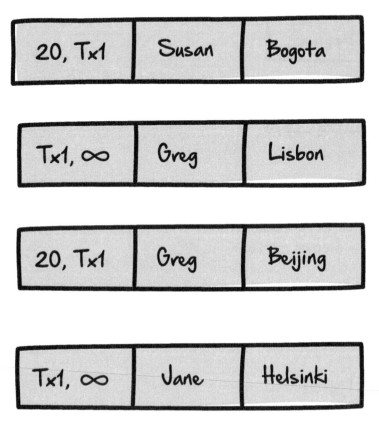

Figure 3-3:   Row versions during an in-flight data modification transaction, Tx1.

During processing, SQL Server uses the `Transaction-ID` for the `Begin-Ts` value of any row it needs to insert, and for the `End-Ts` value for any row that it needs to mark for deletion. SQL Server uses an extra bit flag to indicate to other transactions that these are transaction ids, not timestamps.

So, to delete the <Susan, Bogota> row (remember, the row isn't actually removed during processing; it's more a case of marking it as deleted), transaction Tx1 first locates the row, via one of the indexes, and then sets the `End-Ts` value to the `Transaction-ID` for Tx1.

The update of <Greg, Beijing> occurs in an atomic step consisting of two separate operations that will delete the original row, and insert a completely new row. Tx1 constructs the new row <Greg, Lisbon>, storing the transaction ID, Tx1, in `Begin-Ts`, and then setting `End-Ts` to ∞ (infinity). As part of the same atomic action, Tx1 deletes the <Greg, Beijing> row, just as described previously. Finally, it inserts the new <Jane, Helsinki> row.

At this stage our transaction, Tx1, issues a `COMMIT`. SQL Server generates the commit timestamp, at 120, say, and stores this value in the global transaction table. This timestamp identifies the point in the serialization order of the database where this transaction's updates have logically all occurred. It does not yet write it to the row header because SQL Server has yet to validate the transaction (more on this shortly), and so has not hardened the transaction to the log, on disk. As such, the transaction is not yet "guaranteed;" it could still abort and roll back, and SQL Server will not acknowledge the commit to the user until validation completes. However, SQL Server will optimistically assume that the transaction *will* actually commit, and makes the row available to other transactions as soon it receives the `COMMIT`.

Avoiding read-write conflicts without locks

Let's discuss what happens if another transaction, Tx2, wants to read the rows in our table, either before Tx1 issued the commit, or after it issued the commit, but before SQL Server has completed its validation of Tx1.

To avoid read-write conflicts when accessing disk-based tables, if a reader attempts to access a row that a writer is updating, the reader will be blocked as soon as it encounters the writer's lock, and so will have to wait for the lock-holder to complete processing and validate. In contrast, thanks to the MVCC model, the same reader of a memory-optimized table simply proceeds processing. Let's examine how that works.

First, let's assume Tx2 starts at timestamp 100, after Tx1 started but before Tx1 issues a COMMIT. Tx2 will read the <Susan, Bogota> row, and find that End-Ts contains a Transaction-ID, Tx1, indicating that the row may have been deleted. Tx2 locates Tx1 in the global transaction table and checks its status to determine if the deletion of <Susan, Bogota> is complete. In our example, Tx1 is still active and so Tx2 can access the <Susan, Bogota> row.

When it accesses the <Greg, Lisbon> row version, Tx2 will see the transaction id in Begin-Ts, check the global transaction table, find Tx1 is still active, follow the index pointer in the header back to the previous row version, and instead return the row version <Greg, Beijing>. Likewise, Tx2 will not return the row <Jane, Helsinki>.

However, what if, instead, we assume Tx2 started at timestamp 121, after Tx1 issued the commit, but *before* SQL Server completed validation of Tx1? If Tx2 started at timestamp 121, then it will be able to access data rows that have a commit timestamp of less than or equal to 121 for Begin-Ts and greater than 121 for End-Ts.

Tx2 reads the <Susan, Bogota> row, finds Tx1 in End-Ts indicating it may be deleted, locates Tx1 in the global transaction table and checks the internal transaction table, where this time it will find the commit timestamp (the "prospective" Begin-Ts value) of 120 for Tx1. The commit for Tx1 is issued but not confirmed (since it hasn't completed validation), but SQL Server optimistically assumes that Tx1 will commit, and therefore that the <Susan, Bogota> row *is* deleted, and Tx2 will not return this row. By a similar argument, it *will* return the rows <Greg, Lisbon>, since prospective Begin-Ts is 120 (=<121) and End-Ts is infinity (>121), and <Jane, Helsinki>.

However, since SQL Server has yet to validate transaction Tx1, it registers a **commit dependency** between Tx2 and Tx1. This means that SQL Server will not complete validation of Tx2, nor acknowledge the commit of Tx2 to the user, until it completes validation of Tx1.

In other words, while a transaction will never be blocked waiting to acquire a lock, it may need to wait a short period for commit dependencies to resolve, during validation.

However, generally, any blocking waits that arise from the resolution of commit dependencies will be minimal. Of course, a "problematic" (e.g. long-running) transaction in an OLTP system is still going to cause some blocking, although never lock-related blocking.

Immediate write-write conflicts

Let's now imagine Tx2, starting at timestamp 100, instead of just reading the rows, wants to update <Greg, Beijing> to <Greg, Porto>. At this stage, the `End-Ts` value for the <Greg, Beijing> row will contain a transaction ID and this, since SQL Server optimistically assumes that Tx1 *will* commit, immediately indicates a write-write conflict, sometimes called an "update conflict," and Tx2 will abort immediately.

This is in contrast to the pessimistic behavior for processing modifications to disk-based tables, where SQL Server will block Tx2 until it can guarantee the commit of Tx1 (or Tx1 rolls back). If Tx1 does commit, Tx2 will see the conflict error; if Tx1 aborts, Tx2 will proceed.

Validation phase

Once our transaction Tx1 issues a commit, and SQL Server generates the commit timestamp, the transaction enters the validation phase. While SQL Server will immediately detect direct update conflicts, such as those discussed in the previous section, it is not until the validation phase that it will detect other potential violations of the properties specified by the transaction isolation level. So, for example, let's say Tx1 was accessing the memory-optimized table in `REPEATABLE READ` isolation. It reads a row value and then Tx2 updates that row value, which it can do because SQL Server acquires no locks in the MVCC model, and issues a `COMMIT` before Tx1 commits. When Tx1 enters the validation phase, it will fail the validation check and SQL Server will abort the transaction. If there are no violations, SQL Server proceeds with other actions that will culminate in guaranteeing the durability of the transaction.

The following summarizes the actions that SQL Server will take during the validation phase (Chapter 5 discusses each of these actions in more detail).

- **Validate the changes made by a transaction** – for example, it will perform checks to ensure that there are no violations of the current transaction isolation level.

- **Wait for any commit dependencies to resolve** (i.e. for the dependency count to reduce to 0).

- **Harden the transaction to disk** – for durable tables only, SQL Server generates a "write set" of changes, basically a list of DELETE/INSERT operations with pointers to the version associated with each operation, and writes it to the transaction log, on disk.

- **Mark the transaction commit as validated**, in the global transaction table.

- **Clear dependencies** of transactions that are dependent on the validated transaction (in our example, once Tx1 validates, Tx2 can now complete validation).

At this stage, Tx1 is validated and it moves to the post-processing stage.

Post-processing

In this stage, SQL Server writes the commit timestamp into the row header of all affected rows (note this is the timestamp from when Tx1 first issued the commit). Therefore, our final row versions look as shown in in Figure 3-4.

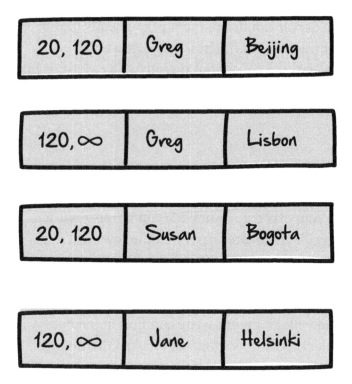

Figure 3-4:   New row versions, after Tx 1 is fully committed.

As noted earlier, the storage engine has no real notion of row "versions." There is no implicit or explicit reference that relates one version of a given row to another. There are just rows, connected together by the table's indexes, as we'll see in the next chapter, and visible to active transactions, or not, depending on the validity interval of the row version compared to the logical read time of the accessing transaction.

In Figure 3-4, the rows <Greg, Beijing> and <Susan, Bogota> have a validity interval of 20 to 120 and so any user transaction with a starting timestamp greater than or equal to 20 and less than 120, will still see those row versions. Any transaction with a starting timestamp greater than 120 will see <Greg, Lisbon> and <Jane, Helsinki>.

Eventually, there will be no active transactions for which the rows <Greg, Beijing> and <Susan, Bogota> are still valid, and so SQL Server can delete them permanently (remove the rows from the index chains and de-allocate memory). These "stale" rows may be removed by users' threads or by a separate "garbage collection" thread (we'll cover this in Chapter 5).

Summary

The SQL Server In-Memory OLTP engine supports true optimistic concurrency, via a MVCC, based on in-memory row versioning. This chapter described the row structure that underpins the MVCC model, and then examined how SQL Server maintains multiple row versions, and determines which is the correct row version to access, during concurrent transactions. This model means that SQL Server can avoid read-write conflicts with the need for any locking, and will raise write-write conflicts immediately, rather than after a delay (i.e. rather than blocking for the duration of a lock-holding transaction).

In the next chapter, we'll examine how SQL Server uses indexes to connect all rows that belong to a single in-memory table, as well as to optimize row access.

Additional Resources

- **Hekaton: SQL Server's Memory-Optimized OLTP Engine** – a white paper by Microsoft Research:
  HTTP://TINYURL.COM/LCG5M4X.

- **Table and Row Size in Memory-Optimized Tables**:
  HTTP://TINYURL.COM/LPF4UVS.

Chapter 4: Hash and Range Indexes

The previous chapter discussed data row structure, and how the in-memory OLTP engine maintains row versions, as part of its optimistic MVCC system.

The row header for each data row contains a set of index pointers, one for each index on the table to which the row belongs. Each pointer points to the next logical row in that table, according to the key for that index. As such, it is these indexes that provide order to the rows in a table. There are no other structures for combining rows into a table other than to link them together with the index pointers; there are no data pages that combine sets of data rows into a single structure, which means that all memory-optimized tables must have at least one index.

Beyond this obligatory index, to connect the rows together, we can choose an additional seven indexes, to a maximum of eight indexes on a table in total, consisting of both **hash** and **range** indexes, in order to optimize access paths for that table.

In this chapter, we're going to explore, in a lot more detail, the storage structure of in-memory indexes. We'll start by discussing hash indexes, how SQL Server can use such an index to join together and organize the rows of a table, and then we'll look at the tactical use of these indexes for query optimization.

We'll then move on to discuss, in depth, the range index and its new Bw-tree internal structure, and the internal maintenance that SQL Server performs on these structures to maintain optimum query performance.

Index Basics

To summarize briefly some of what we've discussed about the "rules" governing the use of indexes on memory-optimized tables:

- all memory-optimized tables must have at least one index

- a maximum of 8 indexes per table, including the index supporting the PRIMARY KEY

- no UNIQUE indexes other than for the PRIMARY KEY

- we can't alter a table after creating it, so we must define all indexes at the time we create the memory-optimized table – SQL Server writes the number of index pointers, and therefore number of indexes, into the row header on table creation

- indexes on memory-optimized tables are entirely in-memory structures – SQL Server never logs any changes made to data rows in indexes, during data modification

- during database recovery SQL Server recreates all indexes based on the index definitions. We'll go into detail in Chapter 6, *Logging, Checkpoint, and Recovery*.

With a maximum limit of 8 indexes, all of which we must define on table creation, we must exert even more care than usual to choose the correct and most useful set of indexes.

We discussed earlier in the book how data rows are not stored on pages, so there is no collection of pages or extents, and there are no partitions or allocation units. Similarly, although we do refer to index pages in in-memory range indexes, they are very different structures from their disk-based counterparts.

In disk-based indexes, the pointers locate physical, fixed-size pages on disk. As we modify data rows, we run into the problem of index fragmentation, as gaps appear in pages during DELETEs, and page splits occur during INSERTs and UPDATEs. Once this fragmentation occurs, the I/O overhead associated with reads and writes grows.

By contrast, the concept of fragmentation is meaningless for indexes on memory-optimized tables. The index is entirely in-memory and SQL Server can read from one memory address just as fast as another, regardless of its exact location in memory. As such, there is no maintenance that a DBA will be required to perform on these indexes. Range indexes do require internal maintenance as rows are added and updated, but these operations are handled automatically by the in-memory OLTP engine. The section on range indexes later in this chapter describes in detail the process by which SQL Server keeps these indexes organized.

Hash Indexes

A hash index, which is stored as a hash table, consists of an array of pointers, where each element of the array is called a **hash bucket** and stores a pointer to the location in memory of a data row. When we create a hash index on a column, SQL Server applies a hash function to the value in the index key column in each row and the result of the function determines which bucket will contain the pointer for that row.

More on hashing

Hashing is a well-known search algorithm, which stores data based on a hash key generated by applying a hash function to the search key (in this case, the index key). A hash table can be thought of as an array of "buckets," one for each possible value that the hash function can generate, and each data element (in this case, each data row) is added to the appropriate bucket based on its index key value. When searching, the system will apply the same hash function to the value being sought, and will only have to look in a single bucket. For more information about what hashing and hash searching are all about, take a look at the Wikipedia article at: HTTP://EN.WIKIPEDIA.ORG/WIKI/HASH_FUNCTION.

Let's say we insert the first row into a table and the index key value hashes to the value 4. SQL Server stores a pointer to that row in hash bucket "4" in the array. If a transaction inserts a new row into the table, where the index key value also hashes to "4," it becomes the first row in the chain of rows accessed from hash bucket 4 in the index, and the new row will have a pointer to the original row.

In other words, the hash index accesses, from the same hash bucket, all key values that hash to the same value (have the same result from the hash function), with subsequent rows linked together in a chain, with one row pointing to the next. If there is duplication of key values, the duplicates will always generate the same function result and thus will always be in the same chain. Ideally, there shouldn't be more than one key value in the same hash chain. If two different key values hash to the same value, which means they will end up in the same hash bucket, or they end up in the same bucket because we specified fewer buckets than there are possible hash values for the column data, then this is a hash collision.

Row organization

As discussed previously, SQL Server stores these index pointers in the index pointer array in the row header. Figure 4-1 shows two rows in a hash index on a name column. For this example, assume there is a very simple hash function that results in a value equal to the length of the string in the index key column. The first value of Jane will then hash to 4, and Susan to 5, and so on. In this simplified illustration, different key values (Jane and Greg, for example) will hash to the same bucket, which is a hash collision. Of course, the real hash function is much more random and unpredictable, but I am using the length example to make it easier to illustrate.

The figure shows the pointers from the 4 and 5 entries in the hash index to the rows containing Jane and Susan, respectively. Neither row points to any other rows, so the index pointers in each of the row headers is NULL.

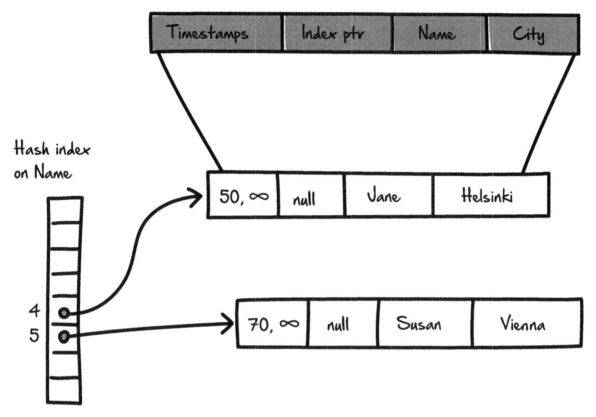

Figure 4-1: A hash index with two rows.

In Figure 4-1, we can see that the <Jane, Helsinki> and <Susan, Vienna> rows have a `Begin-Ts` timestamp of 50 and 70 respectively, and each is the current, active version of that row.

In Figure 4-2, a transaction, which committed at timestamp 100, has added to the same table a row with a `name` value of Greg. Using our string length hash function, Greg hashes to 4, and so maps to the same bucket as Jane, and the row is linked into the same chain as the row for Jane. The <Greg, Beijing> row has a pointer to the <Jane, Helsinki> row and SQL Server updates the hash index to point to Greg. The <Jane, Helsinki> row needs no changes.

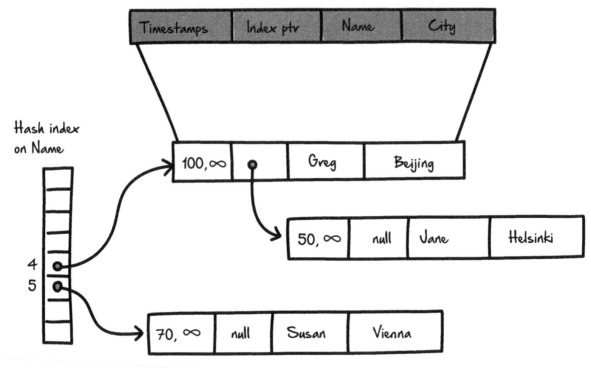

Figure 4-2: A hash index with three rows.

Finally, what happens if another transaction, which commits at timestamp 200, updates <Greg, Beijing> to <Greg, Lisbon>? The new version of Greg's row is simply linked in as any other row, and will be visible to active transactions depending on their timestamps, as described in Chapter 3. Every row has at least one pointer to it, either directly from the hash index bucket or from another row.

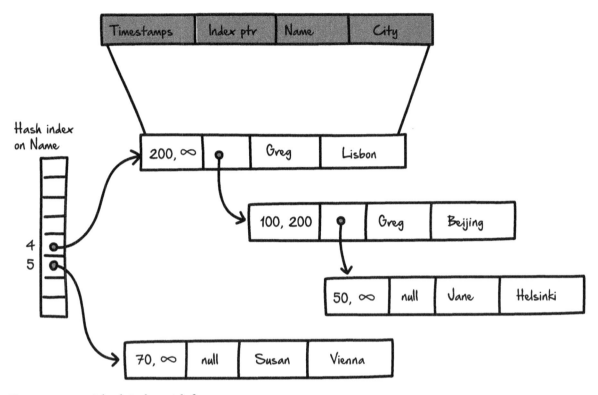

Figure 4-3: A hash index with four rows.

Of course, this is just a simple example with one index, in this case a hash index, which is the minimum required to link the rows together. However, for query performance purposes, we may want to add other hash indexes (as well as range indexes).

For example, if equality searches on the City column are common, and if it were quite a selective column (small number of repeated values), then we might decide to add a hash index to that column, too. This creates a second index pointer field. Each row in the table now has two pointers pointing to it, and can point to two rows, one for each index. The first pointer in each row points to the next value in the chain for the Name index; the second pointer points to the next value in the chain for the City index.

Figure 4-4 shows the same hash index on Name, this time with three rows that hash to 4, and two rows that hash to 5, which uses the second bucket in the Name index. The second index on the City column uses three buckets. The bucket for 6 has three values in the chain, the bucket for 7 has one value in the chain, and the bucket for 8 also has one value.

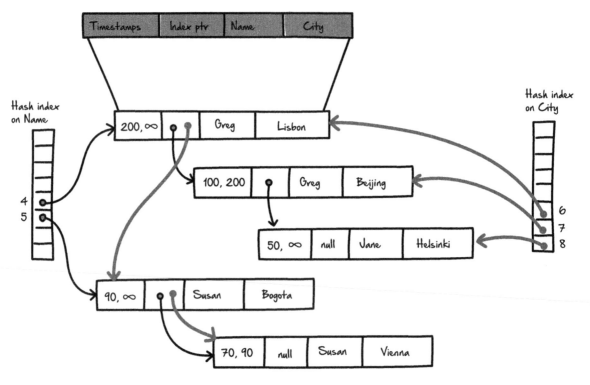

Figure 4-4: Two hash indexes on the same table.

Now we have another access path through the rows, using the second hash index.

Choosing hash indexes

Hash indexes are most effective for performing targeted searches, using equality predicates, on high cardinality columns (small number of repeating values). In many tables, the PRIMARY KEY column will meet these criteria and so the PK index will be a hash index (although, of course, there may also be PKs that we want to search by range).

Hash indexes become less effective on columns that have lots of duplicate values, unless whenever you're querying on that column, you really do want to return all the rows that have that particular value. If SQL Server has to search many duplicate values in a hash chain, but a query only needs a few of the rows that have that value, then performance will be adversely affected due to the cost of traversing the long hash chains. This can happen if a query has filters on multiple columns, but the index is based on only one of the filtered columns. For example, suppose you have both lastname and firstname columns in your table, but an index on lastname only. If you are searching for all the rows where lastname = 'Smith' and firstname = 'Sue', SQL Server will have to search the entire chain of 'Smith' values, and inspect each row to determine if the firstname value is the desired one. The index would be more useful if we needed to return all the rows with the lastname value 'Smith'.

When defining a hash index, bear in mind that the hash function used is based on *all* the key columns. This means that if you have a hash index on the columns: lastname, firstname in an employees table, a row with the values <Harrison, Josh> will have a different value returned from the hash function than <Harrison, John>. This means that a query that just supplies a lastname value, i.e. Harrison, will not be able to use the index at all, since Harrison may appear in many hash buckets. Therefore, in order to "seek" on hash indexes the query needs to provide equality predicates for all of the key columns.

Determining the number of hash buckets

When creating a hash index during table creation, we must specify a number of buckets. For example, Listing 4-1 creates a hash index on our Name column, with 100,000 buckets.

```
CREATE TABLE T1
(
    [Name] varchar(32) not null PRIMARY KEY NONCLUSTERED HASH
                                    WITH (BUCKET_COUNT = 100000),
    [City] varchar(32) null,
    [State_Province] varchar(32) null,
    [LastModified] datetime not null,

) WITH (MEMORY_OPTIMIZED = ON, DURABILITY = SCHEMA_AND_DATA);
```

Listing 4-1:   Defining a hash index.

SQL Server rounds up the number we supply for the BUCKET_COUNT to the next power of two, so it will round up a value of 50,000 to 65,536.

The number of buckets for each hash index should be determined based on the characteristics of the column on which we are building the index. It is recommended to choose a number of buckets equal to or greater than the expected cardinality (i.e. the number of unique values) of the index key column, so that there will be a greater likelihood that each bucket's chain will point to rows with the same value for the index key column. In other words, we want to try to make sure that two different values will never end up in the same bucket. If there are fewer buckets than possible values, multiple values will have to use the same bucket, i.e. a hash collision.

This can lead to long chains of rows and significant performance degradation of all DML operations on individual rows, including SELECT and INSERT. On the other hand, be careful not to choose a number that is too big because each bucket uses memory (8 bytes per bucket). Having extra buckets will not improve performance but will simply waste memory. As a secondary concern, it might also reduce the performance of index scans, which will have to check each bucket for rows.

A new Dynamic Management View (DMV), `sys.dm_db_xtp_hash_index_stats`, provides information on number of buckets and hash chain lengths, which is useful for understanding and tuning the bucket counts. We can also use the view to detect cases where the index key has many duplicates.

If this DMV returns a large average chain length, it indicates that many rows are hashed to the same bucket. This could happen for the following reasons:

- If the number of empty buckets is low or the average and maximum chain lengths are similar, it is likely that the total bucket count is too low. This causes many different index keys to hash to the same bucket.

- If the number of empty buckets is high or the maximum chain length is high relative to the average chain length, it is likely that there are many rows with duplicate index key values or there is a skew in the key values. All rows with the same index key value hash to the same bucket, hence there is a long chain length in that bucket.

Conversely, short chain lengths along with a high empty bucket count are in indication of a `bucket_count` that is too high.

Range Indexes

Hash indexes are useful for relatively unique data that we can query with equality predicates. However, if you don't know the cardinality, and so have no idea of the number of buckets you'll need for a particular column, or if you know you'll be searching your data based on a range of values, you should consider creating a range index instead of a hash index.

Range indexes connect together all the rows of a table at their leaf level. Every row in a table will be accessible by a pointer in the leaf. Range indexes are implemented using a new data structure called a **Bw-tree**, originally envisioned and described by Microsoft Research in 2011. A Bw-tree is a lock- and latch-free variation of a B-tree.

The Bw-tree

The general structure of a Bw-tree is similar to SQL Server's regular B-trees, except that the index pages are not a fixed size, and once they are built they cannot be changed. Like a regular B-tree page, each index page contains a set of ordered key values, and for each value there is a corresponding pointer. At the upper levels of the index, on what are called the **internal pages**, the pointers point to an index page at the next level of the tree, and at the leaf level, the pointers point to a data row. Just like for in-memory OLTP hash indexes, multiple data rows can be linked together. In the case of range indexes, rows that have the same value for the index key will be linked.

One big difference between Bw-trees and SQL Server's B-trees is that, in the former, a page pointer is a logical page ID (PID), instead of a physical page address. The PID indicates a position in a mapping table, which connects each PID with a physical memory address. Index pages are never updated; instead, they are replaced with a new page and the mapping table is updated so that the same PID indicates a new physical memory address.

Figure 4-5 shows the general structure of a Bw-tree, plus the Page Mapping Table.

Each index row in the internal index pages contains a key value, and a PID of a page at the next level down. The index pages show the key values that the index references. Not all the PID values are indicated in Figure 4-5, and the mapping table does not show all the PID values that are in use.

The key value is the highest value possible on the page referenced. Note this is different than a regular B-tree index, for which the index rows stores the **minimum** value on the page at the next level down. The leaf level index pages also contain key values but, instead of a PID, they contain an actual memory address of a data row, which could be the first in a chain of data rows, all with the same key value (these are the same rows that might also be linked using one or more hash indexes).

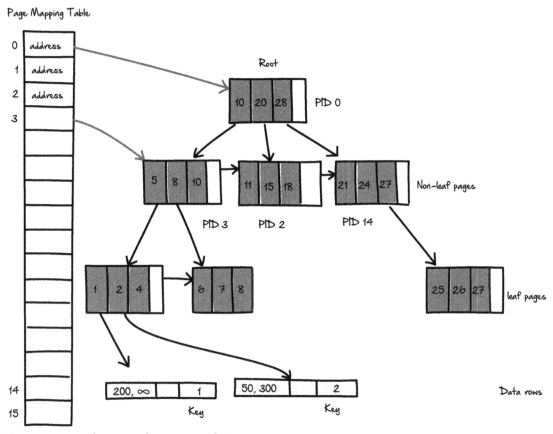

Figure 4-5: The general structure of a Bw-tree.

Another big difference between Bw-trees and SQL Server's B-trees is that, at the leaf level, SQL Server keeps track of data changes using a set of delta values. As noted above, index pages are never updated, they are just replaced with a new page. However, the leaf pages themselves are not replaced for every change. Instead, each update to a leaf-level index page, which can be an insert or delete of a key value on that page, produces a page containing a **delta record** describing the change.

An update is represented by two new delta records, one for the delete of the original value, and one for the insert of the new value. When SQL Server adds each delta record, it updates the mapping table with the physical address of the page containing the newly added delta record for the insert or delete operation.

Figure 4-6 illustrates this behavior. The mapping table is showing only a single page with logical address P. The physical address in the mapping table originally was the memory address of the corresponding leaf level index page, shown as page P. After we insert a new row into the table, with index key value 50 (which we'll assume did not already occur in the table's data), in-memory OLTP adds a delta record linked to page P, indicating the insert of the new key, and the physical address of page P is updated to indicate the address of this first delta record page.

Assume, then, that a separate transaction deletes from the table the only row with index key value 48. In-memory OLTP must then remove the index row with key 48, so it creates another delta record, and once again updates the physical address for page P.

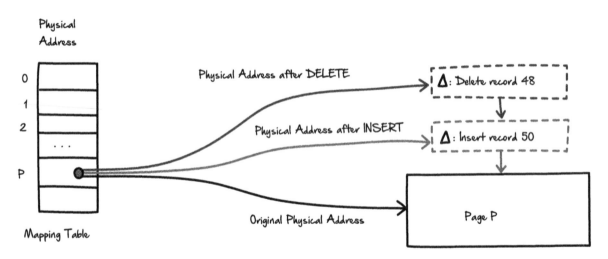

Figure 4-6: Delta records linked to a leaf level index page.

When searching through a range index, SQL Server must combine the delta records with the base page, making the search operation a bit more expensive. However, not having to completely replace the leaf page for every change gives us performance savings. As we'll see in the later section, *Consolidating delta records*, eventually SQL Server will combine the original page and chain of delta pages into a new base page.

Index page structures

In-memory OLTP range index pages are not a fixed size, as they are for indexes on disk-based tables, although the maximum index page size is still 8 KB.

Range index pages for memory-optimized tables all have a header area which contains the following information:

- **PID** – the pointer into the mapping table.

- **Page type** – leaf, internal, delta or special.

- **Right PID** – the PID of the page to the right of the current page.

- **Height** – the vertical distance from the current page to the leaf.

- **Page statistics** – the count of delta records plus the count of records on the page.

- **Max Key** – the upper limit of values on the page.

In addition, both leaf and internal pages contain two or three fixed length arrays:

- **Values** – this is really an array of pointers. Each entry in the array is 8 bytes long. For internal pages, each entry contains the PID of a page at the next level and, for a leaf page, the entry contains the memory address for the first row in a chain of rows having equal key values. (Note that, technically, the PID could be stored in 4 bytes, but to allow the same values structure to be used for all index pages, the array allows 8 bytes per entry.)

- **Keys** – this is the array of key values. If the current page is an internal page, the key represents the first value on the page referenced by the PID. If the current page is a leaf page, the key is the value in the chain of rows.

- **Offsets** – this array exists only for pages of indexes with variable length keys. Each entry is 2 bytes and contains the offset where the corresponding key starts in the key array on the page.

The smallest pages are typically the delta pages, which have a header containing most of the same information as in an internal or leaf page. However delta page headers don't have the arrays described for leaf or internal pages. A delta page contains only an operation code (insert or delete) and a value, which is the memory address of the first row in a chain of records. Finally, the delta page will also contain the key value for the current delta operation. In effect, we can think of a delta page as being a mini-index page holding a single element, whereas the regular index pages store an array of N elements. Remember that the Bw-tree leaf pages contain only pointers to the first row of an index chain, for each key value, not a pointer to every row in the table.

Internal index maintenance operations

There are three different operations that the in-memory OLTP engine may need to perform in order to manage the structure of a Bw-tree: **consolidation**, **split** and **merge**. For all of these operations, it *makes no changes to existing index pages*. Changes may be made to the mapping table to update the physical address corresponding to a PID value. If an index page needs to add a new row, or have a row removed, a whole new internal page is created and the PID values are updated in the mapping table, as described previously.

Consolidating delta records

A long chain of delta records can eventually degrade search performance if SQL Server has to consider the changes in the delta records along with the contents of the index pages when it's searching through an index. If in-memory OLTP attempts to add a new delta record to a chain that already has 16 elements, it will consolidate the changes in the delta records into the referenced index page, and then rebuild the page, which will include the changes indicated by the new delta record that triggered the consolidation. The newly rebuilt index page will have the same PID as the original index page but a new memory address. The old pages (index page plus delta pages) will be marked for garbage collection.

Splitting a full index page

An index page in a Bw-tree grows on an as-needed basis, starting from storing a single row to storing a maximum of 8 KB. Once the index page grows to 8 KB, a new insert of a single row will cause it to split. For an internal page, this means when there is no more room to add another key value and pointer and, for a leaf page, it means that the row would be too big to fit on the page once all the delta records were incorporated.

The statistics information in the page header for a leaf page keeps track of how much space would be required to consolidate the delta records, and that information is adjusted as each new delta record is added. The easiest way to visualize how a page split occurs is to walk through an example. Figure 4-7 shows a representation of the original structure, where P_s is the page to be split into pages P_1 and P_2, and P_p is its parent page, with a row that points to P_s. Keep in mind that a split can happen at any level of an index, so it is not specified whether P_s is a leaf page or an internal page. It could be either.

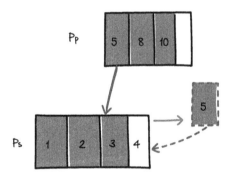

Figure 4-7:   Attempting to insert a new row into a full index page.

Assume we have executed an **INSERT** statement that inserts a row with key value of 5 into this table, so that 5 now needs to be added to the range index. The first entry in page P_p is a 5, which means 5 is the maximum value that could occur on the page to which P_p points, which is P_s. Page P_s doesn't currently have a value 5, but page P_s is where the 5 belongs. However, the page P_s is full, so it is unable to add the key value 5 to the page, and it has to split. The split operation occurs in one atomic operation consisting of two steps, as described in the next two sections.

Step 1: Allocate new pages, split the rows

Step 1 allocates two new pages, P_1 and P_2, and splits the rows from page P_s onto these pages, including the newly inserted row. A new slot in the page mapping table stores the physical address of page P_2. These pages, P_1 and P_2 are not yet accessible to any concurrent operations and those will see the original page, P_s. In addition, the "logical" pointer from P_1 to P_2 is set. Figure 4-8 shows the changes, where P_1 contains key values 1 thru 3 and P_2 contains key values 4 and 5.

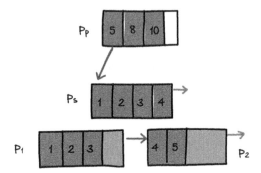

Figure 4-8:   Splitting a full index page into two pages.

In the same atomic operation as splitting the page, SQL Server updates the page mapping table to change the pointer to point to P_1 instead of P_s. After this operation, page P_p points directly to page P_1; there is no pointer to page P_s, as shown in Figure 4-9.

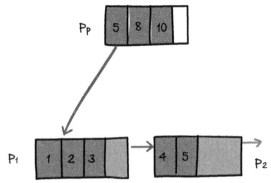

Figure 4-9:   The pointer from the parent points to the first new child page.

Step 2: Create a new pointer

Eventually, all pages should be directly accessible from the higher level but, for a brief period, after Step 1, the parent page P_p points to P_1 but there is no direct pointer from P_p to page P_2, although P_p contains the highest value that exists on P_2, which is 5. P_2 can be reached only via page P_1.

To create a pointer from P_p to page P_2, SQL Server allocates a new parent page P_{pp}, copies into it all the rows from page P_p, and adds a new row to point to page P_1, which holds the maximum key value of the rows on P_1 which is 3, as shown in Figure 4-10.

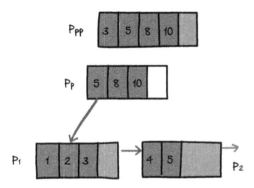

Figure 4-10:   A new parent page is created.

In the same atomic operation as creating the new pointer, SQL Server then updates the page mapping table to change the pointer from P_p to P_{pp}, as shown in Figure 4-11.

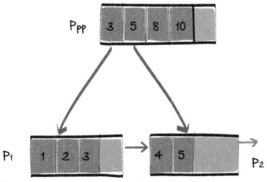

Figure 4-11:   After the split is complete.

Merging adjacent index pages

When a DELETE operation leaves an index page P with less than 10% of the maximum page size (currently 8 KB), or with a single row on it, SQL Server will merge page P with its neighboring page. When a row is deleted from page P, SQL Server adds a new delta record for the delete, as usual, and then checks to see if the remaining space after deleting the row will be less than 10% of maximum page size. If it will be, then page P qualifies for a merge operation.

Again, to illustrate how this works, we'll walk through a simple example, which assumes we'll be merging a page P with its left neighbor, Page P_{ln}, that is, one with smaller values.

Figure 4-12 shows a representation of the original structure where page P_p, the parent page, contains a row that points to page P. Page P_{ln} has a maximum key value of 8, meaning that the row in page P_p that points to page P_{ln} contains the value 8. We will delete from page P the row with key value 10, leaving only one row remaining, with the key value 9.

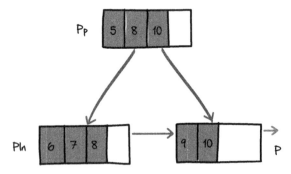

Figure 4-12: Index pages prior to deleting Row 10.

The merge operation occurs in three atomic steps, as described over the following sections.

Step 1: Create new delta pages for delete

SQL Server creates a delta page, DP_{10}, representing key value 10 and its pointer is set to point to page P. Additionally, SQL Server creates a special "merge-delta page," DP_m, and links it to point to DP_{10}. At this stage, neither DP_{10} nor DP_m are visible to any concurrent transactions.

In the same atomic step, SQL Server updates the pointer to page P in the page mapping table to point to DP_m. After this step, the entry for key value 10 in parent page P_p now points to DP_m.

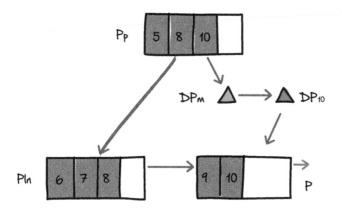

Figure 4-13:   The delta page and the merge-delta page are added to indicate a deletion.

Step 2: Create a new non-leaf page with correct index entries

In Step 2, SQL Server removes the row with key value 8 in page P_p (since 8 will no longer be the high value on any page) and updates the entry for key value 10 (DP_{10}) to point to page P_{ln}. To do this, it allocates a new non-leaf page, P_{p2}, and copies to it all the rows from P_p except for the row representing key value 8.

Once this is done, in the same atomic step, SQL Server updates the page mapping table entry pointing to page P_p to point to page P_{p2}. Page P_p is no longer reachable.

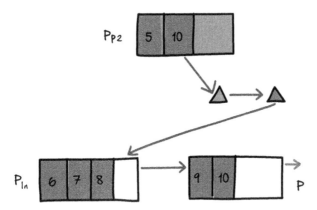

Figure 4-14: Pointers are adjusted to get ready for the merge.

Step 3: Merge pages, remove deltas

In the final step, SQL Server merges the leaf pages P and P_{ln} and removes the delta pages. To do this, it allocates a new page, P_{new}, merges the rows from P and P_{ln}, and includes the delta page changes in the new P_{new}. Finally, in the same atomic operation, SQL Server updates the page mapping table entry currently pointing to page P_{ln} so that it now points to page P_{new}. At this point, the new page is available to any concurrent transactions.

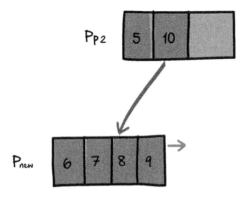

Figure 4-15: After the merge is completed.

Summary

Memory-optimized tables comprise individual rows connected together by indexes. This chapter described the two index structures available: hash indexes and range indexes.

Hash indexes have a fixed number of buckets, each of which holds a pointer to a chain of rows. Ideally, all the rows in a single bucket's chain will have the same key value, and the correct choice for the number of buckets, which is declared when the table is created, can help ensure this.

Range indexes are stored as Bw-trees, which are similar to SQL Server's traditional B-trees in some respects, but very different in others. The internal pages in Bw-trees contain key values and pointers to pages and the next level. The leaf level of the index contains pointers to chains of rows with matching key values. Just like for our data rows, index pages are never updated in place. If an index page needs to add or remove a key value, a new page is created to replace the original.

When choosing the correct set of indexes for a table at table creation time, evaluate each indexed column to determine the best type of index. If the column stores lots of duplicate values, or queries need to search the column by a range of values, then a range index is the best choice. Otherwise, choose a hash index.

In the next chapter we'll look at how concurrent operations are processed and how transactions are managed and logged.

Additional Resources

- **Guidelines for Using Indexes on Memory-Optimized Tables**:
  HTTP://TINYURL.COM/M9J4Q37.

- **The Bw-Tree: A B-tree for New Hardware Platforms**:
  HTTP://TINYURL.COM/PVD5FDK.

Chapter 5: Transaction Processing

Regardless of whether we access disk-based tables or memory-optimized tables, SQL Server must manage concurrent transactions against these tables in a manner that preserves the ACID properties of every transaction. Every transaction runs in a particular transaction isolation level, which determines the degree to which it is isolated from the effects of changes made by the concurrent transactions of other users.

In this chapter, we'll discuss transaction management for memory-optimized tables, and the isolation levels supported for operations on memory-optimized tables. We'll also explore the possible validation errors that can occur, and describe how SQL Server In-Memory OLTP deals with them.

Transaction Scope

SQL Server supports several different types of transaction, in terms of how we define the beginning and end of the transaction; and when accessing memory-optimized tables the transaction type can affect the isolation levels that SQL Server supports. The two default types of transactions are:

- **explicit** transactions – use the `BEGIN TRANSACTION` statement to indicate the beginning of the transaction, and either a `COMMIT TRANSACTION` or a `ROLLBACK TRANSACTION` statement to indicate the end. In between, the transaction can include any number of statements.

- **autocommit** transactions – any single data modification operation. In other words, any `INSERT`, `UPDATE` or `DELETE` statement (as well as others, such as `MERGE` and `BULK INSERT`), by itself, is automatically a transaction. If we modify one row, or one million rows, in a single `UPDATE` statement, SQL Server will consider the `UPDATE` operation to be an atomic operation, and will modify either all the rows or none of them. With an auto-commit transaction, there is no way to force a rollback, manually. A transaction rollback will only occur when there is a system failure.

In addition, we can also define a non-default type of transaction called an **implicit** transaction, invoked under the session option `SET IMPLICIT_TRANSACTIONS ON`. In implicit transaction mode, the start of any transaction is implied. In other words, any data manipulation language (DML) statement (such as `INSERT`, `UPDATE`, `DELETE` and even `SELECT`) will automatically start a transaction. The end of the transaction must still be explicit, and the transaction is not finished until we issue either a `ROLLBACK TRAN` or `COMMIT TRAN`.

Transaction Isolation Levels

A transaction's isolation level determines its sensitivity to the changes made by other concurrent transactions. Before we look at the details of isolation levels, we need to understand some basic properties that determine what we mean by **data consistency**. The most important properties that we may wish SQL Server to enforce for our transactions are as follows:

- **Read stability** – a transaction, TxA, reads some version, v1, of a record during processing. To achieve read stability, SQL Server must guarantee that v1 is still the version visible to TxA as of the end of the transaction; that is, v1 has not been replaced by another committed version, v2. SQL Server enforces read stability either by acquiring a shared lock on v1, to prevent changes, or by validating that no other transaction updated v1 before TxA committed.

- **Phantom avoidance** – to achieve phantom avoidance, SQL Server must be able to guarantee that consecutive scans performed by transaction TxA would not return additional new versions added between the time TxA starts and the time TxA commits. SQL Server can enforce phantom avoidance in two ways: by locking the scanned part of an index/table, or by rescanning before the transaction is committed to check for new versions.

If these properties are not enforced, certain read phenomena can occur, such as non-repeatable reads and phantoms. In some situations, dirty reads can also occur, although dirty reads are not possible when working with memory-optimized tables in SQL Server.

Isolation levels are defined in terms of read phenomena. In other words, transaction TxA's isolation level determines which read phenomena are acceptable and, therefore, what measures SQL Server must take to prevent changes made by other transactions from introducing these phenomena into the results of transaction TxA.

In a pessimistic concurrency model, such as when accessing disk-based tables, SQL Server acquires locks to prevent "interference" between concurrent transactions, in this way avoiding these read phenomena. Generally speaking, the more restrictive the isolation level (i.e. the fewer read phenomena it allows) the more restrictive SQL Server's locking regime will be, and the higher the risk of blocking, as sessions wait to acquire locks.

By contrast, SQL Server regulates all access of data in memory-optimized tables using completely optimistic MVCC. SQL Server does not use locking or latching to provide transaction isolation, and so data operations never wait to acquire locks. Instead, SQL Server assumes that concurrent transactions won't interfere and then performs validation checks once a transaction issues a commit to ensure that it obeys the required isolation properties. If it does, then SQL Server will confirm the commit.

SQL Server still supports multiple levels of transaction isolation when assessing memory-optimized tables, but there are differences in the way the isolation levels are guaranteed when accessing disk-based versus memory-optimized tables.

First, for comparative purposes, let's review briefly the transaction isolation levels that SQL Server supports when accessing disk-based tables, and then contrast that to the isolation levels we can use with memory-optimized tables and how they work.

Isolation levels with disk-based tables

SQL Server, when accessing disk-based tables, supports the following transaction isolation levels, listed from least- to most-restrictive and describing briefly how SQL Server implements each level for disk-based table access.

- **READ UNCOMMITTED** – allows dirty reads, non-repeatable reads and phantom reads (this level in not recommended and we won't discuss it further).

- **READ COMMITTED** – prevents dirty reads, allows non-repeatable reads and phantom reads.

  - To support the standard implementation of this isolation level, for disk-based tables, transactions must acquire a shared read lock to read a row, and release it as soon as the read is complete (although the transaction as a whole may still be incomplete) and so can't perform dirty reads. Transactions hold exclusive locks until the end of the transaction.

  - SQL Server also offers a snapshot-based implementation of the same READ COMMITTED isolation level (called READ_COMMITTED_SNAPSHOT) for disk-based tables. It uses row versioning in tempdb, rather than locks.

- **SNAPSHOT** – guarantees that data read by any statement in a transaction will be the transactionally-consistent version of the data that existed at the start of the transaction. In other words, the statements in a snapshot transaction see a snapshot of the committed data as it existed at the start of the transaction. Any modifications made after that are invisible to it. It does not prevent non-repeatable reads or phantoms, but they won't appear in the results, so this level has the outward appearance of SERIALIZABLE. For disk-based tables, SQL Server implements this level, using row versioning in tempdb.

- **REPEATABLE READ** – *prevents* dirty reads and non-repeatable reads but allows phantom reads. Transactions take shared locks and exclusive locks until the end of the transaction to guarantee read stability.

- **SERIALIZABLE** – *prevents* all read phenomena. To avoid phantoms, SQL Server adopts a special locking mechanism, using key-range locks, and holds all locks until the end of the transaction, so that other transactions can't insert new rows into those ranges.

Isolation levels with memory-optimized tables

SQL Server supports the following transaction isolation levels for transactions accessing memory-optimized tables:

- **SNAPSHOT** – a transaction running in snapshot isolation will always see the most recent committed data. Does not *guarantee* read stability or phantom avoidance, though queries running in this isolation level won't *see* any non-repeatable reads or phantoms.

- **REPEATABLE READ** – includes the guarantees given by SNAPSHOT plus read stability. Every read operation in the transaction is repeatable up to the end of the transaction.

- **SERIALIZABLE** – includes the guarantees of REPEATABLE READ isolation level plus phantom avoidance. Guarantees that a query will see exactly the same data if all its reads were repeated at the end of the transaction.

Since in-memory OLTP uses a completely optimistic concurrency model, SQL Server implements each of the levels very differently than for disk-optimized table access, without using any locks or latches.

When accessing memory-optimized tables, SQL Server ensures read stability if required by the isolation level, by validating that a row version read by a query in transaction T1, during processing, has not been modified by another transaction, before T1 committed. It ensures phantom avoidance, as required, by rescanning during transaction validation, to check for new "phantom" row versions that were inserted before T1 committed. We'll discuss what happens when violations occur, a little later in the chapter.

When accessing memory-optimized tables from interpreted T-SQL, we must specify the isolation level using a table-level hint, or via a new database option called `MEMORY_OPTIMIZED_ELEVATE_TO_SNAPSHOT`. For a natively compiled stored procedure, we must specify the transaction isolation level as part of an `ATOMIC` block (we'll discuss this in more detail in Chapter 7).

All of the examples in this chapter will access memory-optimized tables from interpreted T-SQL.

Rules for cross-container transactions (interpreted T-SQL)

When we execute interpreted T-SQL to access memory-optimized tables, in general we need to specify a supported transaction isolation level, using a table hint, or use the `MEMORY_OPTIMIZED_ELEVATE_TO_SNAPSHOT` database option.

Any transaction that we execute from interpreted T-SQL can access both disk-based and memory-optimized tables (whereas a natively compiled stored procedure can only access memory-optimized tables), and so we refer to it as a cross-container transaction.

There are strict rules that govern the isolation level combinations we can use when accessing disk-based and memory-optimized tables, in order that SQL Server can continue to guarantee transactional consistency. Most of the restrictions relate to the fact that operations on disk-based tables and operations on memory-optimized tables each have their own transaction sequence number, even if they are accessed in the same T-SQL transaction. You can think of a cross-container transaction as having two sub-transactions within the larger transaction: one sub-transaction is for the disk-based tables and one is for the memory-optimized tables.

Table 5-1 lists which isolation levels can be used together in a cross-container transaction.

Disk-based tables	Memory-optimized tables	Recommendations
READ COMMITTED	SNAPSHOT	This is the baseline combination and should be used for most situations using READ COMMITTED for disk-based tables.
READ COMMITTED	REPEATABLE READ / SERIALIZABLE	This combination can be used during data migration and for memory-optimized table access in interop mode (not in a natively compiled procedure).
REPEATABLE READ / SERIALIZABLE	SNAPSHOT	This combination can be useful during migration and if no concurrent write operations are being performed on the memory-optimized tables.
SNAPSHOT		No memory-optimized table access allowed.
REPEATABLE READ / SERIALIZABLE	REPEATABLE READ / SERIALIZABLE	This combination is not allowed.

Table 5-1:   Compatible isolation levels in cross-container transactions.

The following sections will explain the restrictions, and the reasons for them, with examples.

READ COMMITTED cross-container transactions must specify a valid isolation level

To follow along with the examples, recreate the memory-optimized table, T1, in our existing HKDB database.

```
USE HKDB
GO
IF EXISTS (SELECT * FROM sys.objects WHERE name='T1')
     DROP TABLE [dbo].[T1]
GO

CREATE TABLE T1
(
   [Name] varchar(32) not null PRIMARY KEY NONCLUSTERED HASH
                                    WITH (BUCKET_COUNT = 100000),
   [City] varchar(32) null,
   [State_Province] varchar(32) null,
   [LastModified] datetime not null,

) WITH (MEMORY_OPTIMIZED = ON, DURABILITY = SCHEMA_AND_DATA);
GO
```

Listing 5-1:   Recreate memory-optimized table, T1.

Open a new query window in SSMS, and start an explicit transaction accessing a memory-optimized table, as shown in Listing 5-2.

```
USE HKDB;
BEGIN TRAN;
SELECT  *
FROM    [dbo].[T1]
COMMIT TRAN;
```

Listing 5-2:   Explicit transaction against T1.

By default, this transaction will run in the READ COMMITTED isolation level, which is the standard isolation level for most SQL Server transactions, and guarantees that the transaction will not read any dirty (uncommitted) data. If a transaction running under this default isolation level tries to access a memory-optimized table, it will generate the following error message, since READ COMMITTED is unsupported for memory-optimized tables:

> Accessing memory optimized tables using the READ COMMITTED isolation level is supported only for autocommit transactions. It is not supported for explicit or implicit transactions. Provide a supported isolation level for the memory optimized table using a table hint, such as WITH (SNAPSHOT).

As the message suggests, the transaction needs to specify a supported isolation level, using a table hint. For example, Listing 5-3 specifies the snapshot isolation level. This combination, READ COMMITTED for accessing disk-based tables and SNAPSHOT for memory-optimized, is the one that most cross-container transactions should use. However, alternatively, we could also use the WITH (REPEATABLEREAD) or WITH (SERIALIZABLE) table hints, if required.

```
USE HKDB;
BEGIN TRAN;
SELECT  * FROM [dbo].[T1] WITH (SNAPSHOT);
COMMIT TRAN;
```

Listing 5-3:   Explicit transaction using a table hint to specify snapshot isolation.

SQL Server does support READ COMMITTED isolation level for auto-commit (single-statement) transactions, so we can run Listing 5-4, inserting three rows into our table T1 successfully.

```
INSERT  [dbo].[T1]
        ( Name, City, LastModified )
VALUES  ( 'Jane', 'Helsinki', CURRENT_TIMESTAMP ),
        ( 'Susan', 'Vienna', CURRENT_TIMESTAMP ),
        ( 'Greg', 'Lisbon', CURRENT_TIMESTAMP );
```

Listing 5-4:   READ COMMITTED isolation is supported only for auto-commit transactions.

Technically, for a single-statement transaction accessing a memory-optimized table, there is no behavioral difference between READ COMMITTED and SNAPSHOT, so we could actually think of these single statements as running in snapshot isolation level.

Likewise, for cross-container transactions, SQL Server supports the snapshot implementation of **READ COMMITTED**, i.e. **READ_COMMITTED_SNAPSHOT**, only for auto-commit transactions, and then only if the query does not access any disk-based tables.

SNAPSHOT cross-container transactions cannot access memory-optimized tables

If our cross-container transaction accesses disk-based tables with **SET TRANSACTION ISOLATION LEVEL SNAPSHOT**, then it simply cannot access memory-optimized tables, regardless of what we attempt with table hints.

```
ALTER DATABASE HKDB
SET ALLOW_SNAPSHOT_ISOLATION ON;

SET TRANSACTION ISOLATION LEVEL SNAPSHOT
USE HKDB;
BEGIN TRAN;
SELECT  *
FROM    [dbo].[T1] WITH ( REPEATABLEREAD );
COMMIT TRAN;

SET TRANSACTION ISOLATION LEVEL READ COMMITTED;

ALTER DATABASE HKDB
SET ALLOW_SNAPSHOT_ISOLATION OFF;
```

Listing 5-5: Attempting to access a memory-optimized table using **SNAPSHOT** isolation.

We see the message:

```
Msg 41332, Level 16, State 0, Line 7
Memory optimized tables and natively compiled stored procedures cannot be accessed or created
when the session TRANSACTION ISOLATION LEVEL is set to SNAPSHOT.
```

For snapshot isolation, all operations need to see the versions of the data that existed as of the beginning of the transaction. For SNAPSHOT transactions, the beginning of the transaction is considered to be when the first table is accessed. In a cross-container transaction, however, since the sub-transactions can each start at a different time, another transaction may have changed data between the start times of the two sub-transactions. The cross-container transaction then will have no one point in time on which to base the snapshot, so using transaction isolation level SNAPSHOT is not allowed.

REPEATABLE READ or SERIALIZABLE cross-container transactions must use SNAPSHOT

Transactions that are started using interpreted T-SQL with either REPEATABLE READ or SERIALIZABLE isolation must access memory-optimized tables using snapshot isolation.

```
SET TRANSACTION ISOLATION LEVEL REPEATABLE READ;
USE HKDB;
BEGIN TRAN;
SELECT  *
FROM    [dbo].[T1];
COMMIT TRAN;
```

Listing 5-6:   Attempting to access a memory-optimized table using REPEATABLE READ isolation.

We see the message:

```
The following transactions must access memory optimized tables and natively compiled stored
procedures under snapshot isolation: RepeatableRead transactions, Serializable transactions,
and transactions that access tables that are not memory optimized in RepeatableRead or
Serializable isolation.
```

Table 5-2 shows an example of running the two cross-container transactions, Tx1 and Tx2 (both of which we can think of as having two "sub-transactions," one for accessing disk-based and one for accessing memory-optimized tables). It illustrates why a transaction can't use REPEATABLE READ or SERIALIZABLE to access both disk-based and memory-optimized tables, and it essentially boils down to the fact that SQL Server implements the isolation levels in very different ways in memory-optimized tables, without using any locks.

In Table 5-2, RHk# indicates a row in a memory-optimized table, and RSql# indicates a row in a disk-based table. Transaction Tx1 reads a row from a memory-optimized table first. SQL Server acquires no locks. Now assume the second transaction, Tx2, starts after Tx1 reads RHk1. Tx2 reads and updates RSql1 and then reads and updates RHk1, then commits. Now when Tx1 read the row from the disk-based table, it would now have a set of values for the two rows that could never have existed if the transaction were run in isolation, i.e. if the transaction were truly serializable, and so this combination is not allowed.

Time	Tx1 (SERIALIZABLE)	Tx2 (any isolation level)
1	BEGIN SQL/in-memory sub-transactions	
2	Read RHk1	
3		BEGIN SQL/in-memory sub-transactions
4		Read RSql1 and update to RSql2
5		Read RHk1 and update to RHk2
6		COMMIT
7	Read RSql2	

Table 5-2:   Two concurrent cross-container transactions.

If a cross-container transaction accesses disk-based tables with REPEATABLE READ or SERIALIZABLE then it can only access memory-optimized tables with snapshot isolation, so that it can still guarantee read stability and phantom avoidance when the

sub-transactions start at different points in time. Therefore, we need to specify the
WITH (SNAPSHOT) hint.

```
SET TRANSACTION ISOLATION LEVEL REPEATABLE READ;
USE HKDB;
BEGIN TRAN;
SELECT  *
FROM    [dbo].[T1]WITH ( SNAPSHOT );
COMMIT TRAN;

SET TRANSACTION ISOLATION LEVEL READ COMMITTED;
```

Listing 5-7: A REPEATABLE READ transaction accessing a T1 using snapshot isolation.

Choosing an isolation level for accessing memory-optimized tables

The simplest and most widely used isolation level for use with memory-optimized tables
and MVCC is snapshot isolation. Remember that snapshot isolation does not guarantee
read consistency or phantom avoidance, only that a transaction will see a consistent view
of the data as of the time the transaction started, and therefore won't see the effects of
any actions that could cause non-repeatable reads or phantoms.

Since snapshot isolation is the recommended isolation level in most cases, a new
database property is available to automatically upgrade the isolation to SNAPSHOT,
for all operations on memory-optimized tables, if the T-SQL transaction is running in
a lower isolation level, i.e. READ COMMITTED, which is SQL Server's default (or READ
UNCOMMITTED, which is not recommended). Listing 5-8 shows an example of setting
this option.

```
ALTER DATABASE HKDB
SET MEMORY_OPTIMIZED_ELEVATE_TO_SNAPSHOT ON;
```

Listing 5-8: Setting the database option to elevate isolation level to SNAPSHOT.

We can verify whether this option has been set in two ways, shown in Listing 5-9, either by inspecting the **sys.databases** catalog view or by querying the **DATABASEPROPERTYEX** function.

```
SELECT   is_memory_optimized_elevate_to_snapshot_on
FROM     sys.databases
WHERE    name = 'HKDB';

SELECT   DATABASEPROPERTYEX('HKDB',
                    'IsMemoryOptimizedElevateToSnapshotEnabled');
```

Listing 5-9:   Verifying if the database has been set to elevate the isolation level to SNAPSHOT.

Otherwise, as demonstrated earlier, simply set the required isolation level on the fly, using a table hint. We should also consider that having accessed a table in a cross-container transaction using an isolation level hint, a transaction should continue to use that same hint for all subsequent access of the table, though this is not enforced. Using different isolation levels for the same table, whether a disk-based table or memory-optimized table, will usually lead to failure of the transaction.

Monitoring Active Transactions

The **sys.dm_db_xtp_transactions** DMV is useful for monitoring in-progress transactions. We can think of this view as allowing us to peek into the global transaction table that we discussed in Chapter 3.

Start two simple transactions doing **INSERT**s into a memory-optimized table, and then run the query in Listing 5-10.

```
SELECT   xtp_transaction_id ,
         transaction_id ,
         session_id ,
         begin_tsn ,
         end_tsn ,
         state_desc
FROM     sys.dm_db_xtp_transactions
WHERE    transaction_id > 0;
GO
```

Listing 5-10: Monitoring transactions on memory-optimized tables.

The output should look similar to that shown in Figure 5-1, with two transactions.

	xtp_transaction_id	transaction_id	session_id	begin_tsn	end_tsn	state_desc
1	1159	132760	54	4	0	ACTIVE
2	1162	132823	58	4	0	ACTIVE

Figure 5-1:   Sample output from the sys.dm_db_xtp_transactions DMV.

When the first statement accessing a memory-optimized table is executed, SQL Server obtains a transaction id for the T-SQL part of the transaction (transaction_id) and a transaction id for the in-memory OLTP portion (xtp_transaction_id).

The xtp_transaction_id values, generated by the Transaction-ID counter (see Chapter 3) are consecutive. It is this value that SQL Server inserts into End-Ts for rows that an active transaction is deleting, and into Begin-Ts for rows that an active transaction is inserting. We can also see that both of these transactions have the same value for begin_tsn, which is the current timestamp for the last committed transaction at the time the transaction started. Since both transactions are still active, there is no value for the end_tsn timestamp. The begin_tsn timestamp is only important while the transaction is running and is never saved in row versions, whereas the end_tsn, upon commit, is the value written into the Begin-Ts and End-Ts for the affected rows.

Transaction Processing Examples

Let's now look at an example DML operation. Assume we have a transaction, Tx1 (we'll use Tx1 as the Transaction-ID), accessing a memory-optimized table using the snapshot isolation level, which starts at timestamp 240 and performs two operations:

- DELETE the row <Greg , Lisbon>.

- UPDATE <Jane, Helsinki> to <Jane, Perth>.

The starting timestamp of 240 indicates when it began relative to the serialization order of the database. While active, it will only be able to access rows that have a Begin-Ts of less than or equal to 240 and an End-Ts of greater than 240.

Open a window in SSMS and execute Listing 5-11 (don't commit the transaction yet).

```
USE HKDB;
BEGIN TRAN Tx1;
DELETE   FROM dbo.T1 WITH ( SNAPSHOT )
WHERE    Name = 'Greg';
UPDATE   dbo.T1 WITH ( SNAPSHOT )
SET      City = 'Perth'
WHERE    Name = 'Jane';
-- COMMIT TRAN Tx1
```

Listing 5-11:   Tx1 deletes one row and updates another.

During the processing phase, SQL Server links the new <Jane, Perth> row into the index structure and marks the <Greg, Lisbon> and <Jane, Helsinki> as deleted. Figure 5-2 shows what the rows will look at this stage, within our index structure (with hash indexes on Name and City; see Chapter 4).

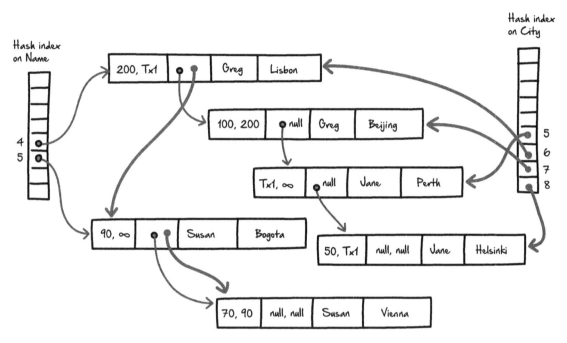

Figure 5-2: Row versions and indexes.

I've just used Tx1 for the `transaction-id`, but you can use Listing 5-10 to find the real values of `xtp_transaction_id`.

Write-write conflicts

What happens if another transaction, TxU, tries to update Jane's row (remember Tx1 is still active)?

```
USE HKDB;
BEGIN TRAN TxU;
UPDATE  dbo.T1 WITH ( SNAPSHOT )
SET     City = 'Melbourne'
WHERE   Name = 'Jane';
COMMIT TRAN TxU
```

Listing 5-12: TxU attempts to update a row while Tx1 is still uncommitted.

103

TxU's session will instantly see the following message:

```
Msg 41302, Level 16, State 110, Line 3
The current transaction attempted to update a record that has been updated since this
transaction started. The transaction was aborted.
Msg 3998, Level 16, State 1, Line 1
Uncommittable transaction is detected at the end of the batch. The transaction is rolled
back.
The statement has been terminated.
```

As discussed in Chapter 3, TxU sees Tx1's `transaction-id` in the <Jane, Helsinki> row and, because SQL Server optimistically assumes Tx1 will commit, immediately aborts TxU, raising a conflict error.

Read-Write conflicts

If a query tries to update a row that has already been updated by an active transaction, SQL Server generates an immediate "update conflict" error. However, SQL Server does not catch most other isolation level errors until the transaction enters the **validation phase**. Remember, no transaction acquires locks so it can't block other transactions from accessing rows. We'll discuss the validation phase in more detail in the next section, but it is during this phase that SQL Server will perform checks to make sure that any changes made by concurrent transactions do not violate the specified isolation level. Let's continue our example, and see the sort of violation that can occur.

Our original Tx1 transaction, which started at timestamp 240, is still active, and let's now start two other transactions that will read the rows in table `T1`:

- Tx2 – an auto-commit, single-statement `SELECT` that starts at timestamp 243.

- Tx3 – an explicit transaction that reads a row and then updates another row based on the value it read in the `SELECT`; it starts at a timestamp of 246.

Tx2 starts before Tx1 commits, and Tx3 starts before Tx2 commits. Figure 5-3 shows the rows that exist after each transaction commits.

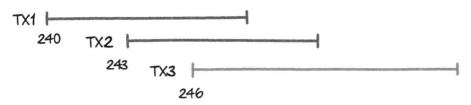

Figure 5-3:   Version visibility after each transaction ends, but before validation.

When Tx1 starts at timestamp 240, three rows are visible, and since Tx1 does not commit until timestamp 250, after Tx2 and Tx3 have started, those are the rows all three of the transactions see. After Tx1 commits, there will only be two rows visible, and the City value for Jane will have changed. When Tx3 commits, it will attempt to change the City value for Susan to Helsinki.

In a second query window in SSMS, we can run our auto-commit transaction, Tx2, which simply reads the T1 table.

```
USE HKDB;
SELECT  Name ,
        City
FROM    T1;
```

Listing 5-13:   Tx2 runs a single-statement SELECT.

Figure 5-4 shows the data that Tx2 returns.

	Name	City
1	Susan	Vienna
2	Jane	Helsinki
3	Greg	Lisbon

Figure 5-4: Tx2 returns three rows.

Tx2's session is running in the default isolation level, **READ COMMITTED**, but as described previously, for a single-statement transaction accessing a memory-optimized table, we can think of Tx2 as running in snapshot isolation level, which for a single-statement **SELECT** will give us the same behavior as **READ COMMITTED**.

Tx2 started at timestamp 243, so it will be able to read rows that existed at that time. It will not be able to access <Greg, Beijing>, for example, because that row was valid between timestamps 100 and 200. The row <Greg, Lisbon> is valid starting at timestamp 200, so transaction Tx2 can read it, but it has a transaction-id in **End-Ts** because Tx1 is currently deleting it. Tx2 will check the global transaction table and see that Tx1 has not committed, so Tx2 can still read the row. <Jane, Perth> is the current version of the row with "Jane," but because Tx1 has not committed, Tx2 follows the pointer to the previous row version, and reads <Jane, Helsinki>.

Tx3 is an explicit transaction that starts at timestamp 246. It will run using **REPEATABLE READ** isolation, and read one row and update another based on the value read, as shown in Listing 5-14 (again, don't commit it yet).

```
DECLARE @City NVARCHAR(32);
BEGIN TRAN TX3
SELECT   @City = City
FROM     T1 WITH ( REPEATABLEREAD )
WHERE    Name = 'Jane';
UPDATE   T1 WITH ( REPEATABLEREAD )
SET      City = @City
WHERE    Name = 'Susan';
COMMIT TRAN  -- commits at timestamp 260
```

Listing 5-14: Tx3 reads the value of City for "Jane" and updates the "Susan" row with this value.

In Tx3, the **SELECT** will read the row <Jane, Helsinki> because that row still is accessible as of timestamp 243. It will then delete the <Susan, Bogota> and insert the row <Susan, Helsinki>.

What happens next depends on which of Tx1 or Tx3 commits first. In our scheme from Figure 5-3, Tx1 commits first. When Tx3 tries to commit after Tx1 has committed, SQL Server will detect during the validation phase that the <Jane, Helsinki> row has been updated by another transaction. This is a violation of the requested **REPEATABLE READ** isolation, so the commit will fail and transaction Tx3 will roll back.

To see this in action, commit Tx1, and then try to commit Tx3. You should see the following error message:

```
Msg 41305, Level 16, State 0, Line 0
The current transaction failed to commit due to a repeatable read validation failure.
```

So Tx1 commits and Tx3 aborts and, at this stage, the only two rows visible will be <Susan, Vienna> and <Jane, Perth>.

If Tx3 had committed before Tx1, then both transactions would succeed, and the final rows visible would be <Jane, Perth> and <Susan, Helsinki>, as shown in Figure 5-3.

Let's now take a look in a little more detail at other isolation level violations that may occur in the validation stage, and at the other actions SQL Server performs during this phase.

Validation Phase

Once a transaction issues a commit and SQL Server generates the commit timestamp, but prior to the final commit of transactions involving memory-optimized tables, SQL Server performs a validation phase. As discussed briefly in Chapter 3, this phase consists broadly of the following three steps:

1. Validate the changes made by Tx1 – verifying that there are no isolation level violations.

2. Wait for any commit dependencies to reduce the dependency count to 0.

3. Log the changes.

Once it logs the changes (which are therefore guaranteed), SQL Server marks the transaction as committed in the global transaction table, and then clears the dependencies of any transactions that are dependent on Tx1.

Note that the only waiting that a transaction on memory-optimized tables will experience is during this phase. There may be waiting for commit dependencies, which are usually very brief, and there may be waiting for the write to the transaction log. Logging for memory-optimized tables is much more efficient than logging for disk-based tables (as we'll see in Chapter 6), so these waits can also be very short.

The following sections review each of these three steps in a little more detail.

Validation phase, Step 1: Check for isolation level violations

SQL Server acquires no locks during data modifications, so it is possible that the data changes of concurrent transactions could result in invalid data, based on the requested isolation level. This step of the commit processing makes sure that there is no invalid data.

During transaction processing, the in-memory OLTP engine will, depending on the isolation level, keep track of the **read-set** and **write-set** for each transaction; these are sets of pointers to the rows that have been read or written, respectively. SQL Server will use the read-set to check for non-repeatable reads, (we'll cover the write-set in the logging section, shortly). Also, depending on the isolation level, it will keep track of a **scan-set**, which is information about the predicate used to access a set of records. SQL Server can use this to check for phantoms.

Table 5-3 summarizes which isolation levels require SQL Server to maintain a read-set or scan-set, or both. Note that for snapshot isolation, it doesn't matter what happens to the data a transaction has read, it only matters that our transaction sees the appropriate data, as of the beginning of the transaction.

Isolation level	Read-set	Scan-set
SNAPSHOT	NO	NO
REPEATABLE READ	YES	NO
SERIALIZABLE	YES	YES

Table 5-3:   Changes monitored in the allowed isolation levels.

SNAPSHOT isolation level violations

If a transaction accesses memory-optimized tables in snapshot isolation, it can encounter a validation error in the following situation:

- Tx1 starts and inserts a row

- Tx2 starts and inserts a row with the same primary key value

- Tx2 commits

- Tx1 commits – encounters validation error.

Table 5-4 illustrates this **SNAPSHOT** isolation failure.

Time	Transaction Tx1	Transaction Tx2
I	BEGIN TRAN	
2	INSERT INTO [dbo].[T1] WITH (SNAPSHOT) (Name, City, LastModified) VALUES ('Bob', 'Basingstoke', CURRENT_TIMESTAMP)	BEGIN TRAN
3		INSERT INTO [dbo].[T1] WITH (SNAPSHOT)(Name, City, LastModified) VALUES ('Bob', 'Bognor', CURRENT_TIMESTAMP)
4		COMMIT TRAN

Time	Transaction Tx1	Transaction Tx2

5	`COMMIT TRAN`
	
	`Error 41325: The current transaction failed to commit due to a serializable validation failure`	

Table 5-4: A snapshot isolation validation error.

During validation, Error 41325 is generated, because we can't have two rows with the same primary key value, and Tx1 is aborted and rolled back.

REPEATABLE READ isolation level violations

For a **REPEATABLE READ** transaction, the transaction's read-set is used to determine if any of the rows read previously have a new version by the end of the transaction.

If a transaction accesses memory-optimized tables in **REPEATABLE READ** isolation, it can encounter the 41325 validation error, as described previously, and also a 41305 error, on attempting to commit, if the current transaction has read any row that was then updated by another transaction that committed before the current transaction.

```
Error 41305: The current transaction failed to commit due to a repeatable read
validation failure.
```

The transaction will abort. We saw an example of this earlier, in the section on read-write conflicts.

SERIALIZABLE isolation level violations

SERIALIZABLE transactions can encounter both 41325 and 41305 validation errors in the situation described previously. In addition, if a transaction accesses memory-optimized tables in SERIALIZABLE isolation, SQL Server uses the transaction's scan-set to determine if any additional rows now meet the predicate's condition. It can encounter a 41325 validation error, upon commit, if the current transaction fails to read a valid row that meets the specified filter conditions (due to deletions by other transactions), or encounters phantoms rows inserted by other transactions that meet the specified filter conditions. The commit will fail. The transaction needs to be executed as if there are no concurrent transactions. All actions logically happen at a single serialization point. If any of these guarantees are violated, error 41325 (shown previously) is generated and the transaction will be aborted.

Time	Transaction Tx1 (SERIALIZABLE)	Transaction Tx2 (any isolation level)
1	BEGIN TRAN	
2	SELECT Name FROM Person WHERE City = 'Perth'	BEGIN TRAN
3		INSERT INTO Person VALUES ('Charlie', 'Perth')
4	--- other operations	
5		COMMIT TRAN
6	COMMIT TRAN During validation, Error 41325 is generated and Tx1 is rolled back	

Table 5-5: Transactions resulting in a SERIALIZABLE isolation failure.

Validation phase, Step 2: Commit dependencies

During regular processing, a transaction can read rows written by other transactions that have issued a commit, but are in the validation or post-processing phases, so SQL Server has yet to confirm the commit.

Since SQL Server assumes that these transactions will actually commit, it generates the logical end timestamps as soon as the commit is issued, which marks the start of the validation phase. These rows are therefore visible to any transaction that started after this time. No transaction will ever be able to see the effects of a transaction that has not entered its validation phase.

If a transaction Tx1 reads rows that Tx2 has updated, and Tx2 is still in the validation phase, then Tx1 will take a commit dependency on Tx2 and increment an internal counter that keeps track of the number of commit dependencies for Tx1. In addition, Tx2 will add a pointer from Tx1 to a list of dependent transactions that Tx2 maintains.

Waiting for commit dependencies to clear has two main implications:

- A transaction cannot commit until the transactions it depends on have committed. In other words, it cannot enter the commit phase until all dependencies have cleared and the internal counter has been decremented to 0.

- In addition, result sets are not returned to the client until all dependencies have cleared. This prevents the client from retrieving uncommitted data.

If any of the dependent transactions fails to commit, there is a commit dependency failure. This means the transaction will fail to commit with the following error:

```
Error 41301: A previous transaction that the current transaction took a dependency on has
aborted, and the current transaction can no longer commit.
```

Note that Tx1 can only acquire a dependency on Tx2 when Tx2 is in the validation or post-processing phase and, because these phases are typically extremely short, commit dependencies will be quite rare in a true OLTP system. If you want to be able to determine if you have encountered such dependencies, you can monitor two extended events. The event `dependency_acquiredtx_event` will be raised when Tx1 takes a dependency on Tx2, and the event `waiting_for_dependenciestx_event` will be raised when Tx1 has explicitly waited for a dependency to clear.

Validation phase, Step 3: Logging

If the any of the modified tables were created with **SCHEMA_AND_DATA**, SQL Server must log the changes to harden them to disk. In-memory OLTP will read the **write-set** for the transaction to determine what operations will be logged.

Transactions track all of their changes in the write-set, which is basically a list of **DELETE/INSERT** operations with pointers to the version associated with each operation. This write-set forms the content of the log for the transaction. Transactions normally generate only a single log record that contains its ID and commit timestamp and the versions of all records it deleted or inserted. There will not be separate log records for each row affected, as there are for disk-based tables. However, there is an upper limit on the size of a log record, and if a transaction on memory-optimized tables exceeds the limit, there can be multiple log records generated.

Figure 5-5 shows the write-set for transaction Tx1, from our previous example in this chapter, in the green box.

Once the log record has been hardened to storage the state of the transaction is changed to `committed` in the global transaction table.

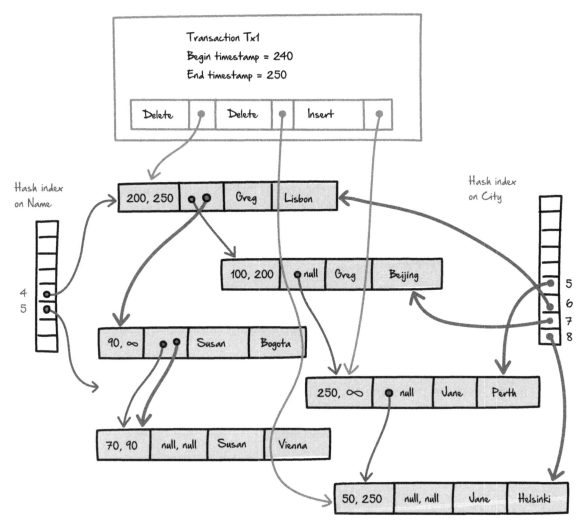

Figure 5-5: Multiple versions of rows after data modifications.

The final step in the validation process is to go through the linked list of dependent transactions and reduce their dependency counters by one. Once this validation phase is finished, the only reason that this transaction might fail is due to a log write failure. Once the log record has been hardened to storage, the state of the transaction is changed to `committed` in the global transaction table.

Post-processing

The final phase is the post-processing, which is sometimes referred to as commit processing, and is usually the shortest. The main operations are to update the timestamps of each of the rows inserted or deleted by this transaction.

- For a **DELETE** operation, set the row's **End-Ts** value to the commit timestamp of the transaction, and clear the type flag on the row's **End-Ts** field to indicate it is really a timestamp, and not a transaction-ID.

- For an **INSERT** operation, set the row's **Begin-Ts** value to the commit timestamp of the transaction and clear the type flag.

If the transaction failed or was explicitly rolled back, inserted rows will be marked as garbage and deleted rows will have their end-timestamp changed back to infinity.

The actual unlinking and deletion of old row versions is handled by the garbage collection system. This final step of removing any unneeded or inaccessible rows is not always done immediately and may be handled either by user threads, once a transaction completes, or by a completely separate garbage collection thread.

Garbage Collection of Rows in Memory

In-memory OLTP is a multi-versioning system, so **DELETE** and **UPDATE** operations (as well as aborted **INSERT** operations) will generate row versions that will eventually become stale, which means they will no longer be visible to any transaction. These unneeded row versions will slow down scans of index structures and create unused memory that needs to be reclaimed.

Garbage collection of checkpoint files

Chapter 6 covers cleanup of checkpoint files – a completely separate process, but also referred to as "garbage collection."

The garbage collection process for stale row versions in memory-optimized tables is analogous to the version store cleanup that SQL Server performs when transactions use one of the snapshot-based isolation levels, when accessing disk-based tables. A big difference though is that the cleanup is not done in tempdb because the row versions are not stored there, but in the in-memory table structures themselves.

To determine which rows can be safely deleted, the in-memory OLTP engine keeps track of the timestamp of the oldest active transaction running in the system, and uses this value to determine which rows are potentially still needed. Any rows that are not valid as of this point in time, in other words any rows with an End-Ts timestamp that is earlier than this time, are considered *stale*. Stale rows can be removed and their memory can be released back to the system.

The garbage collection system is designed to be non-blocking, cooperative and scalable. Of particular interest is the "cooperative" attribute. Although there is a dedicated system thread for the garbage collection process, called the **idle worker** thread, user threads actually do most of the work.

If, while scanning an index during a data modification operation, (all index access on memory-optimized tables is considered to be scanning), a user thread encounters a stale row version, it will either mark the row as expired, or unlink that version from the current chain and adjust the pointers. For each row it unlinks, it will also decrement the reference count in the row header area (reflected in the IdxLinkCount value).

When a user thread completes a transaction, it adds information about the transaction to a queue of transactions to be processed by the idle worker thread. Each time the garbage collection process runs, it processes the queue of transactions, and determines whether the oldest active transaction has changed.

It moves the transactions that have committed into one or more "worker" queues, sorting the transactions into "generations" according to whether or not it committed before or after the oldest active transaction. (We can view the transactions in each generation using the `sys.dm_db_xtp_gc_cycle_stats` DMV, for which see Chapter 8.) It groups the rows associated with transactions that committed before the oldest active transaction into "work items," each consisting of a set of 16 "stale" rows that are ready for removal. The final act of a user thread, on completing a transaction, is to pick up one or more work items from a worker queue and perform garbage collection, i.e. free the memory used by the rows making up the work items.

The idle worker thread will dispose of any stale rows that were eligible for garbage collection, but not accessed by a user transaction, as part of what is termed a "dusty corner" scan. Every row starts with a reference value of 1, so the row can be referenced by the garbage collection mechanism even if the row is no longer connected to any indexes. The garbage collector process is considered the "owner" of the initial reference.

The garbage collection thread processes the queue of completed transactions about once a minute, but the system can adjust the frequency internally, based on the number of completed transactions waiting to be processed. As noted above, each work item it adds to the worker queue currently consists of a set of 16 rows, but that number is subject to change in future versions. These work items are distributed across multiple worker queues, one for each CPU used by SQL Server.

The DMV `sys.dm_db_xtp_index_stats` has a row for each index on each memory-optimized table, and the column `rows_expired` indicates how many rows have been detected as being stale during scans of that index. There is also a column called `rows_expired_removed` that indicates how many rows have been unlinked from that index. As mentioned above, once rows have been unlinked from all indexes on a table, it can be removed by the garbage collection thread. So you will not see the `rows_expired_removed` value going up until the `rows_expired` counters have been incremented for every index on a memory-optimized table.

The query in Listing 5-15 allows us to observe these values. It joins the **sys.dm_db_xtp_ index_stats** DMV with the **sys.indexes** catalog view to be able to return the name of the index.

```
SELECT   name AS 'index_name' ,
         s.index_id ,
         scans_started ,
         rows_returned ,
         rows_expired ,
         rows_expired_removed
FROM     sys.dm_db_xtp_index_stats s
         JOIN sys.indexes i ON s.object_id = i.object_id
                           AND s.index_id = i.index_id
WHERE    OBJECT_ID('<memory-optimized table name>') = s.object_id;
GO
```

Listing 5-15: Observing the process of garbage collection.

Depending on the volume of data changes and the rate at which new versions are generated, SQL Server can be using a substantial amount of memory for old row versions and we need to make sure that our system has enough memory available. I'll tell you more about memory management for a database supporting memory-optimized tables in Chapter 8.

Summary

This chapter contains a lot of detail on the transaction isolation levels that SQL Server supports when accessing memory-optimized tables, and also on the valid combination of levels for cross-container transactions, which can access both disk-based and memory-optimized tables. In most cases, our cross-container transactions will use standard READ COMMITTED for accessing disk-based tables, and SNAPSHOT isolation for memory-optimized tables, set either via a table hint or using the MEMORY_OPTIMIZED_ELEVATE_ TO_SNAPSHOT database property for that database.

In the MVCC model, no transaction acquires locks, and no transaction can prevent another transaction reading, or attempting to modify, rows that it is currently accessing. Due to the optimistic model, SQL Server will raise an immediate conflict if one transaction tries to modify a row that another active transaction is already modifying. However, it will only detect other read-write conflicts during a validation phase which occurs after a transaction issues a commit. We investigated the sort of violations that can occur during validation, depending on the isolation levels being used, and we also considered what happens during other phases of the validation cycle, such as resolving commit dependencies and hardening the log records to disk. Finally, we discussed the cooperative garbage collection system that disposes of stale rows which are no longer visible to any transactions.

We're now ready to take a closer look at the processes by which in-memory OLTP writes to durable storage, namely the CHECKPOINT process and the transaction logging process.

Additional Resources

- **General background on isolation levels**:
  HTTP://EN.WIKIPEDIA.ORG/WIKI/ISOLATION_(DATABASE_SYSTEMS).

- **A Critique of ANSI SQL Isolation Levels**:
  HTTP://TINYURL.COM/LBGSSTL.

- **Understanding Transactions on Memory-Optimized Tables**:
  HTTP://TINYURL.COM/LTQPZOB.

Chapter 6: Logging, Checkpoint, and Recovery

SQL Server must ensure transaction durability for memory-optimized tables, so that it can guarantee to recover to a known state after a failure. In-memory OLTP achieves this by having both the checkpoint process and the transaction logging process write to durable storage.

The information that SQL Server writes to disk consists of transaction log streams and checkpoint streams:

- **Log streams** contain the changes made by committed transactions logged as insertion and deletion of row versions.

- **Checkpoint streams** come in two varieties:

  - **data streams** contain all versions inserted during a timestamp interval

  - **delta streams** are associated with a particular data stream and contain a list of integers indicating which versions in its corresponding data stream have been deleted.

The combined contents of the transaction log and the checkpoint streams are sufficient to allow SQL Server to recover the in-memory state of memory-optimized tables to a transactionally-consistent point in time.

Although the overall requirement for the checkpoint and transaction logging process to write to durable storage is no different than for normal disk-based tables, for in-memory tables the mechanics of these processes are rather different, and often much more efficient, as we'll discuss throughout this chapter.

Though not covered in this book, in-memory OLTP is also integrated with the AlwaysOn Availability Group feature, and so supports fail-over and recovery to highly available replicas.

Transaction Logging

The log streams contain information about all versions inserted and deleted by transactions against in-memory tables. SQL Server writes the log streams to the regular SQL Server transaction log, but in-memory OLTP's transaction logging is designed to be more scalable and higher performance than standard logging for disk-based tables.

Scalability: multiple concurrent log streams

When logging for disk-based tables, SQL Server relies on the ordering of log records in the transaction log (i.e. on the Log Sequence Number, the LSN), to determine the serialization order, so it must write all log records to the end (the "tail") of the log. Even if we create (say) four log files for a database, SQL Server will write log records to Log File 1 until it is full, then fill File 2, and so on. In a database subject to a high level of writes, the need to write all log records to a single place can become a scaling bottleneck.

By contrast, in-memory OLTP relies solely on the transaction end timestamps (End-Ts, see Chapter 3) to determine the serialization order, so it is designed to support multiple, concurrently-generated log streams per database. In theory, this removes the potential scaling bottleneck. However, for SQL Server 2014, the in-memory OLTP integration with SQL Server makes use of only a single log stream per database, because SQL Server supports only one log per database. In other words, SQL Server currently treats the log as one logical file even if multiple physical log files exist. In current testing, this has not been a problem because in-memory OLTP generates much less log data and fewer log writes compared with operations on disk-based tables.

Performance: reduced logging

Given the same workload, SQL Server will write far fewer log records for an in-memory table than for its equivalent disk-based table. There are several reasons for this. One is that it does not log any operations on indexes on memory-optimized tables (it simply rebuilds all indexes during recovery). A second reason is that, rather than write every atomic change as a single log record as for disk-based tables, in-memory OLTP will combine many changes into a single log record. Each transaction is logged in a minimal number of potentially large log records.

A third and critical reason is that in-memory OLTP never writes to disk log records associated with uncommitted transactions. Let's look at this last point in a little more detail, and contrast it to the logging behavior for disk-based tables.

During a modification to a disk-based table, SQL Server constructs log records describing the change as the modification proceeds, writing them to the log buffer in memory, before it modifies the corresponding data pages in memory. When a transaction issues a commit, SQL Server flushes the log buffer to disk, and this will also flush log records relating to any concurrent, as-yet-uncommitted transactions. However, it doesn't write the data pages till later, on checkpoint. If SQL Server crashes after a transaction, T_1, commits but before a checkpoint, the log contains the redo information needed to persist the effects of T_1 during recovery.

By contrast, for memory-optimized tables, the in-memory OLTP engine only constructs the log records for a transaction at the point that it issues the commit, so it will never flush to disk log records relating to uncommitted transactions. At commit, SQL Server combines the changes into a few relatively large log records and writes them to disk. In-memory OLTP does harden the log records to disk before any data is written to disk. In fact, the checkpoint files get the rows to write from the hardened log. Therefore, it can always redo the effects of a transaction, should SQL Server crash before the checkpoint operation occurs.

When working with disk-based tables, a checkpoint flushes to disk *all* dirty pages in memory. A dirty page is any page in the cache that has changed since SQL Server read it from disk or since the last checkpoint, so that the page in cache is different from what's on disk. This is not a selective flushing; SQL Server flushes out all dirty pages, regardless of whether they contain changes associated with open (uncommitted) transactions. However, the Write Ahead Logging (WAL) mechanism used by the log buffer manager guarantees to write the log records to disk *before* it writes the dirty data pages to the physical data files. Therefore if SQL Server crashes immediately after a checkpoint, during recovery it can guarantee to "undo" the effects of any transactions for which there is no "commit" log record.

By contrast, for in-memory OLTP, all data modifications are in-memory; it has no concept of a "dirty page" that needs to be flushed to disk and, since it generates log records only at commit time, checkpoint will never write to disk log records related to uncommitted transactions. So, while the transaction log contains enough information about committed transactions to redo the transaction, no undo information is written to the transaction log, for memory-optimized tables.

In order to demonstrate the greatly reduced logging for memory-optimized tables over disk-based tables, the simple script in Listing 6-1 creates a database, with a single memory-optimized filegroup holding a single container. As always, you may need to edit the file paths to reflect drives and folders available to you, or you may need to create a new folder. I am using a single data folder, C:\DataHK\.

```
USE master
GO
IF DB_ID('LoggingDemo')IS NOT NULL
    DROP DATABASE LoggingDemo;
GO
CREATE DATABASE LoggingDemo ON
    PRIMARY (NAME = [LoggingDemo_data],
      FILENAME = 'C:\DataHK\LoggingDemo_data.mdf'),
      FILEGROUP [LoggingDemo_FG] CONTAINS MEMORY_OPTIMIZED_DATA
```

```
          (NAME = [LoggingDemo_container1],
           FILENAME = 'C:\DataHK\LoggingDemo_container1')
    LOG ON (name = [LoggingDemo_log],
            Filename='C:\DataHK\LoggingDemo.ldf', size= 100 MB);
GO
```

Listing 6-1:   Create the LoggingDemo database.

Listing 6-2 creates one memory-optimized table, and the equivalent disk-based table, in the LoggingDemo database.

```
USE LoggingDemo
GO
IF OBJECT_ID('t1_inmem') IS NOT NULL
     DROP TABLE [dbo].[t1_inmem]
GO

-- create a simple memory-optimized table
CREATE TABLE [dbo].[t1_inmem]
   ( [c1] int NOT NULL,
     [c2] char(100) NOT NULL,
     CONSTRAINT [pk_index91] PRIMARY KEY NONCLUSTERED HASH ([c1])
                                   WITH(BUCKET_COUNT = 1000000)
   ) WITH (MEMORY_OPTIMIZED = ON,
           DURABILITY = SCHEMA_AND_DATA);
GO

IF OBJECT_ID('t1_disk') IS NOT NULL
     DROP TABLE [dbo].[t1_disk]
GO
-- create a similar disk-based table
CREATE TABLE [dbo].[t1_disk]
   ( [c1] int NOT NULL,
     [c2] char(100) NOT NULL)
GO
CREATE UNIQUE NONCLUSTERED INDEX t1_disk_index on t1_disk(c1);
GO
```

Listing 6-2:   Create the t1_inmem and t1_disk tables.

Next, Listing 6-3 populates the disk-based table with 100 rows, and examines the contents of the transaction log using the undocumented (and unsupported) function `fn_dblog()`. You should see 200 log records for operations on `t1_disk`.

```
SET NOCOUNT ON;
GO
BEGIN TRAN
DECLARE @i INT = 0
WHILE ( @i < 100 )
    BEGIN
        INSERT  INTO t1_disk
        VALUES  ( @i, REPLICATE('1', 100) )
        SET @i = @i + 1
    END
COMMIT

-- you will see that SQL Server logged 200 log records
SELECT  *
FROM    sys.fn_dblog(NULL, NULL)
WHERE   PartitionId IN ( SELECT partition_id
                         FROM   sys.partitions
                         WHERE  object_id = OBJECT_ID('t1_disk') )
ORDER BY [Current LSN] ASC;
GO
```

Listing 6-3: Populate the disk-based table with 100 rows and examine the log.

Listing 6-4 runs a similar **INSERT** on the memory-optimized table. Note that, since the `partition_id` is not shown in the output for memory-optimized tables, we cannot filter based on the specific object. Instead, we need to look at the most recent log records, so the query performs a descending sort based on the LSN.

```
BEGIN TRAN
DECLARE @i INT = 0
WHILE ( @i < 100 )
    BEGIN
        INSERT  INTO t1_inmem
        VALUES  ( @i, REPLICATE('1', 100) )
        SET @i = @i + 1
    END
COMMIT
-- look at the log
SELECT  *
FROM    sys.fn_dblog(NULL, NULL)
ORDER BY [Current LSN] DESC;
GO
```

Listing 6-4: Examine the log after populating the memory-optimized tables with 100 rows.

You should see only three log records related to this transaction, as shown in Figure 6-1, one marking the start of the transaction, one the commit, and then just one log record for inserting all 100 rows.

	Current LSN	Operation	Context	Transaction ID	LogBl
1	00000020:00000157:0006	LOP_COMMIT_XACT	LCX_NULL	0000:00000323	0
2	00000020:00000157:0005	LOP_HK	LCX_NULL	0000:00000323	0
3	00000020:00000157:0004	LOP_BEGIN_XACT	LCX_NULL	0000:00000323	0

Figure 6-1: SQL Server transaction log showing one log record for a 100-row transaction.

The output implies that all 100 inserts have been logged in a single log record, using an operation of type LOP_HK, with LOP indicating a "logical operation" and HK being an artifact from the project codename, Hekaton.

We can use another undocumented, unsupported function to break apart a LOP_HK record, as shown in Listing 6-5 (replace the current LSN value with the LSN for your LOP_HK record).

```
SELECT  [current lsn] ,
        [transaction id] ,
        operation ,
        operation_desc ,
        tx_end_timestamp ,
        total_size ,
        OBJECT_NAME(table_id) AS TableName
FROM    sys.fn_dblog_xtp(NULL, NULL)
WHERE   [Current LSN] = '00000020:00000157:0005';
```

Listing 6-5: Break apart a LOP_HK log record.

The first few rows of output should look similar to those shown in Figure 6-2. It should return 102 rows, including one *_INSERT_ROW operation for each of the 100 rows inserted.

	current lsn	transaction id	operation	operation_desc	tx_end_timestam
1	00000020:00000157:0005	0000:00000323	LOP_HK	HK_LOP_BEGIN_TX	3
2	00000020:00000157:0005	0000:00000323	LOP_HK	HK_LOP_INSERT_ROW	3
3	00000020:00000157:0005	0000:00000323	LOP_HK	HK_LOP_INSERT_ROW	3
4	00000020:00000157:0005	0000:00000323	LOP_HK	HK_LOP_INSERT_ROW	3
5	00000020:00000157:0005	0000:00000323	LOP_HK	HK_LOP_INSERT_ROW	3
6	00000020:00000157:0005	0000:00000323	LOP_HK	HK_LOP_INSERT_ROW	3
7	00000020:00000157:0005	0000:00000323	LOP_HK	HK_LOP_INSERT_ROW	3

Figure 6-2: Breaking apart the log record for the inserts on the memory-optimized table.

The single log record for the entire transaction on the memory-optimized table, plus the reduced size of the logged information, can help to make transactions on memory-optimized tables much more efficient. This is not to say, however, that transactions on memory-optimized tables are *always* going to be more efficient, in terms of logging, than operations on disk-based tables. For very short transactions particularly, disk-based and memory-optimized will generate about the same amount of log. However, transactions on memory-optimized tables should never be any *less* efficient than on their disk-based counterparts.

Checkpoint

The two main purposes of the checkpoint operation, for disk-based tables, are to improve performance by batching up I/O rather than continually writing a page to disk every time it changes, and to reduce the time required to run recovery. If checkpoint ran only very infrequently then, during recovery, there could be a huge number of data rows to which SQL Server needs to apply redo, as a result of committed transactions hardened to the log but where the data pages were not hardened to disk before SQL Server entered recovery.

Similarly, one of the main reasons for checkpoint operations, for memory-optimized tables, is to reduce recovery time. The checkpoint process for memory-optimized tables is designed to satisfy two important requirements:

- **Continuous checkpointing** – checkpoint-related I/O operations occur incrementally and continuously as transactional activity accumulates. This is in contrast to the hyper-active checkpoint scheme for disk-based tables, defined as checkpoint processes which sleep for a while, after which they wake up and work as hard as possible to finish up the accumulated work, and which can potentially be disruptive to overall system performance.

- **Streaming I/O** – on disk-based tables, the checkpoint operation generates random I/O as it writes dirty pages to disk. For memory-optimized tables, checkpointing relies, for most of its operations, on streaming I/O (which is always sequential) rather than random I/O. Even on SSD devices, random I/O is slower than sequential I/O and can incur more CPU overhead due to smaller individual I/O requests.

Since checkpointing is a continuous process for memory-optimized tables, when we talk about a checkpoint "event," we're actually talking about the closing of a checkpoint. The later section, *Closing a checkpoint*, describes exactly what happens during the checkpoint closing process.

A checkpoint event for memory-optimized tables is invoked in these situations:

- **Manual** checkpoint – an explicit `checkpoint` command initiates checkpoint operations on both disk-based tables and memory-optimized tables.

- **Automatic** checkpoint – SQL Server runs the in-memory OLTP checkpoint when the size of the log has grown by 512 MB since the last checkpoint. Note that this is not dependent on the amount of work done on memory-optimized tables, only the size of the transaction log. It's possible that there have been no transactions on memory-optimized tables when a checkpoint event occurs.

Anatomy of checkpoint files

Checkpoint streams are stored in SQL Server `FILESTREAM` files, which in essence are sequential files fully managed by SQL Server. `FILESTREAM` storage was introduced in SQL Server 2008 and in-memory OLTP checkpoint files take advantage of that technology.

Checkpoint data is stored in two types of checkpoint files: data files and delta files. These, plus the log records for transactions affecting memory-optimized tables, are the only physical storage associated with memory-optimized tables. Data and delta files are stored in pairs, sometimes referred to as a **Checkpoint File Pair**, or **CFP**.

A checkpoint **data file** contains only inserted versions or rows, either new rows, generated by `INSERT`s or new versions of existing rows, generated by `UPDATE` operations, as we saw in Chapter 3. Each file covers a specific timestamp range and will contain all rows with a `Begin-Ts` timestamp value that falls within that range. Data files are append-only while they are open and, once closed, they are strictly read-only.

A checkpoint **delta file** stores information about which rows contained in its partner data file have been subsequently deleted. When we delete rows, the checkpoint thread will append a reference to the deleted rows (their IDs) to the corresponding delta files. Delta files are append-only for the lifetime of the data file to which they correspond. At recovery time, the delta file is used as a filter to avoid reloading deleted versions into memory. The valid row versions in the data files are reloaded into memory and re-indexed.

There is a 1:1 correspondence between delta files and data files, and both cover exactly the same timestamp range. Since each data file is paired with exactly one delta file, the smallest unit of work for recovery is a data/delta file pair. This allows the recovery process to be highly parallelizable as transactions can be recovered from multiple CFPs concurrently.

Let's take an initial look, at the file system level, at how SQL Server creates these CFPs. First, create a CkptDemo database, with a single container, as shown in Listing 6-6.

```
USE master
GO
IF DB_ID('CkptDemo') IS NOT NULL
    DROP DATABASE CkptDemo;
GO
CREATE DATABASE CkptDemo ON
   PRIMARY (NAME = [CkptDemo_data], FILENAME = 'C:\DataHK\CkptDemo_data.mdf'),
   FILEGROUP [CkptDemo_FG] CONTAINS MEMORY_OPTIMIZED_DATA
      (NAME = [CkptDemo_container1],
       FILENAME = 'C:\DataHK\CkptDemo_container1')
 LOG ON (name = [CkptDemo_log],
         Filename='C:\DataHK\CkptDemo.ldf', size= 100 MB);
GO
```

Listing 6-6:   Create a new database for memory-optimized tables.

Next, Listing 6-7 turns on an undocumented trace flag, 9851, which inhibits the automatic merging of checkpoint files. This will allow us to control when the merging occurs, and observe the process of creating and merging checkpoint files. Only use this trace flag during testing, not on production servers.

```
DBCC TRACEON (9851, -1);

-- set the database to full recovery.
ALTER DATABASE CkptDemo SET RECOVERY FULL;
GO
```

Listing 6-7: Turn on Trace Flag 9851 to inhibit automatic merging of checkpoint files.

At this point, you might want to look in the folder containing the memory-optimized data files, in this example `DataHK\CkptDemo_container1`. Within that folder is one subfolder called `$FSLOG` and another with a GUID for a name. If we had specified multiple memory-optimized filegroups in Listing 6-5, then we'd see one GUID-named folder for each filegroup.

Open the GUID-named folder, and in there is another GUID-named folder. Again, there will be one GUID-named folder at this level for each file in the filegroup. Open up that GUID-named folder, and you will find it is empty, and it will remain empty until we create a memory-optimized table, as shown in Listing 6-8.

```
USE CkptDemo;
GO
-- create a memory-optimized table with each row of size > 8KB
CREATE TABLE dbo.t_memopt (
        c1 int NOT NULL,
        c2 char(40) NOT NULL,
        c3 char(8000) NOT NULL,
        CONSTRAINT [pk_t_memopt_c1] PRIMARY KEY NONCLUSTERED HASH (c1)
          WITH (BUCKET_COUNT = 100000)
) WITH (MEMORY_OPTIMIZED = ON, DURABILITY = SCHEMA_AND_DATA);
GO
```

Listing 6-8: Create the t_memopt memory-optimized table.

At this point, if we re-examine the previously empty folder, we'll find that it now contains 18 files (9 CFPs), as shown in Figure 6-3. The larger ones are the data files, and the smaller ones are the delta files.

Name ▲	Date modified	Type	Size	
00000021-000000a2-0002	8/19/2014 1:44 PM	File	1,024 KB	
00000021-000000a7-0003	8/19/2014 1:44 PM	File	16,384 KB	
00000021-000000ae-0002	8/19/2014 1:44 PM	File	1,024 KB	
00000021-000000b3-0003	8/19/2014 1:44 PM	File	16,384 KB	
00000021-000000ba-0002	8/19/2014 1:44 PM	File	1,024 KB	
00000021-000000bf-0003	8/19/2014 1:44 PM	File	16,384 KB	
00000021-000000c6-0002	8/19/2014 1:44 PM	File	1,024 KB	
00000021-000000cb-0003	8/19/2014 1:44 PM	File	16,384 KB	
00000021-000000d2-0002	8/19/2014 1:44 PM	File	1,024 KB	
00000021-000000d7-0003	8/19/2014 1:44 PM	File	16,384 KB	
00000021-000000de-0002	8/19/2014 1:44 PM	File	1,024 KB	
00000021-000000e3-0003	8/19/2014 1:44 PM	File	16,384 KB	
00000021-000000ea-0002	8/19/2014 1:44 PM	File	1,024 KB	
00000021-000000ef-0003	8/19/2014 1:44 PM	File	16,384 KB	
00000021-000000f6-0002	8/19/2014 1:44 PM	File	1,024 KB	
00000021-00000077-0048	8/19/2014 1:44 PM	File	16,384 KB	
00000021-00000093-0002	8/19/2014 1:44 PM	File	1,024 KB	
00000021-00000098-0003	8/19/2014 1:44 PM	File	16,384 KB	

Address bar: ▼ Computer ▼ Local Disk (C:) ▼ DataHK ▼ CkptDemo_container1 ▼ 84dde134-4b47-4332-a31a-8ac34f8228ac ▼ 3122049f-13bb-4c25-a8a5-972980337acc

Include in library ▼   Share with ▼   New folder

Figure 6-3:   The data and delta files in the container for our memory-optimized tables.

If we had created multiple containers in the filegroup containing the memory-optimized tables, the checkpoint files would be spread across them. For example, if we had two containers, one would contain the data files and one would contain the delta files. If we had three containers, there would be some of the data files and some of the delta files in each container. It is recommended that you consider having an even number of containers in your database, so that each container has only one kind of file.

Continuous checkpointing and checkpoint events

When we insert a data row into a memory-optimized table, the continuous checkpointing process will append the inserted row to a checkpoint data file for that database. The metadata refers to the CFPs to which the continuous checkpointing process writes as having a STATE of UNDER CONSTRUCTION (more on CFP states shortly).

A checkpoint event will close any currently open (UNDER CONSTRUCTION) data files, and the state of these CFPs transitions to ACTIVE. For memory-optimized tables, we often refer to the checkpoint as a "collection of files," referring to the set of data files that were closed when the checkpoint event occurred, plus their corresponding delta files.

From this point, the continuous checkpointing process will no longer write new INSERTS into the closed data files, but they are still very much active, since current rows in these data files may be subject to DELETE and UPDATE operations, which will be reflected in their corresponding delta files. For example, as the result of an UPDATE, the continuous checkpointing process will mark the current row version as deleted in the delta file of the appropriate ACTIVE CFP, and insert the new row version into the data file of the current UNDER CONSTRUCTION CFP.

Every checkpoint event creates a new set of ACTIVE CFPs and so the number of files can grow rapidly. As data modifications proceed, a "deleted" row remains in the data file but the delta file records the fact that it was deleted. Therefore, over time, the percentage of meaningful content in older ACTIVE data files falls, due to DELETEs and UPDATEs. Eventually, SQL Server will merge adjacent data files, so that rows marked as deleted actually get deleted from the checkpoint data file, and create a new CFP. We'll see how this works in the later section, *Merging checkpoint files*.

At a certain point, there will be no open transactions that could possibly affect the content of a closed but active CFP. This point is reached once the oldest transaction still required by SQL Server (marking the start of the active log, a.k.a. the log truncation point) is more recent than the time range covered by the CFP, and the CFP transitions into non-active states. Finally, assuming a log backup (which requires at least one database backup) has occurred, these CFPs are no longer required and can be removed by the checkpoint file garbage collection process.

Let's take a more detailed look at the various states through which CFPs transition.

CFP metadata states

The checkpoint file pairs can be in one of the following states:

- **PRECREATED** – SQL Server reserves a small set of pre-allocated CFPs, in order to minimize wait time when new files are needed. It creates these files upon creation of the first memory-optimized table, whether or not it contains any data. The PRECREATED files will, of course, contain no data.

  - Generally, PRECREATED files will be full-sized files with a data file size of 128 MB and a delta file size of 8 MB. However, if the machine has less than 16 GB of memory, the data file will be 16 MB and the delta file will be 1 MB.

  - The number of PRECREATED CFPs is equal to the number of logical processors (or schedulers) with a minimum of 8. This gives us a fixed minimum storage requirement in databases with memory-optimized tables.

- **UNDER CONSTRUCTION** – These CFPs are "open" and the continuous checkpointing process writes to these CFPs any newly inserted and possibly deleted data rows, since the last checkpoint.

- **ACTIVE** – These CFPs contain the inserted/deleted rows for the last checkpoint event. The checkpoint event "closes" any CFPs with a current status of UNDER CONSTRUCTION, and their status changes to ACTIVE. The continuous checkpointing process will no longer write to the data files of ACTIVE CFPs, but will, of course, still write to any deletes to the ACTIVE delta files. During a database recovery operation the ACTIVE CFPs contain all inserted/deleted rows that will be required to restore the data, before applying the tail log backup.

- In general, the combined size of the ACTIVE CFPs should be about twice the size of the memory-optimized tables. However, there may be situations, in particular if your database files are larger than 128 MB, in which the merging process (discussed a little later) can lag behind the file creation operations, and the total size of your ACTIVE CFPs may be more than twice the size of the memory-optimized tables.

- **MERGE TARGET** – When currently ACTIVE CFPs are chosen for merging, SQL Server creates a new CFP, which consists of a data file that stores the consolidated rows from the two adjacent data files of the CFPs that the merge policy identified, plus a new (empty) delta file. The resulting new CFP will have the status MERGE TARGET until the merge is installed, when it will transition into the ACTIVE state.

- **MERGED SOURCE** – Once the merge has taken place and the MERGE TARGET CFPs are part of checkpoint, the MERGE TARGET CFPs transition to ACTIVE and the original source CFPs transition to the MERGED SOURCE state.

  - Note that, although the merge policy evaluator may identify multiple possible merges, a CFP can only participate in one merge operation.

- **REQUIRED FOR BACKUP/HA** – Upon a subsequent checkpoint event, the MERGED SOURCE CFPs can transition into the REQUIRED FOR BACKUP/HA state. CFPs in this state must be retained until the next log backup. They are also needed for the operational correctness of a database with memory-optimized tables. One example would be that the files are needed to recover from a checkpoint to go back in time during a restore.

- **IN TRANSITION TO TOMBSTONE** – Once the log truncation point is more recent than the time range covered by a CFP, and a log backup has occurred, the CFPs are no longer needed by the in-memory OLTP engine, so they can they can be garbage collected. This state indicates that these CFPs are waiting for the garbage collection thread to transition them to the TOMBSTONE state.

- **TOMBSTONE** – These CFPs are waiting to be garbage collected by the FILESTREAM garbage collector. We'll discuss garbage collection later in the chapter.

Listing 6-9 shows how to interrogate the checkpoint file metadata, using the **sys.dm_db_xtp_checkpoint_files** DMV. It returns one row for each file, along with property information for each file.

```
SELECT   file_type_desc ,
         state_desc ,
         internal_storage_slot ,
         file_size_in_bytes ,
         inserted_row_count ,
         deleted_row_count ,
         lower_bound_tsn ,
         upper_bound_tsn ,
         checkpoint_file_id ,
         relative_file_path
FROM     sys.dm_db_xtp_checkpoint_files
ORDER BY file_type_desc ,
         state_desc ,
         lower_bound_tsn;
GO
```

Listing 6-9:   Examine the metadata for the checkpoint files.

Listing 6-9 returns the following metadata columns (other columns are available; see the documentation for a full list):

- **file_type_desc**
  Identifies the file as a data or delta file.

- **state_desc**
  The state of the file (see previous bullet list).

- **internal_storage_slot**
  This value is the pointer to an internal storage array (described below), but is not populated until a file becomes **ACTIVE**.

- **file_size_in_bytes**
  Note that we have just two sizes so far; the DATA files are
  16777216 bytes (16 MB) and the delta files are 1048576 bytes (1 MB).

- **inserted_row_count**
  This column is only populated for data files.

- **deleted_row_count**
  This column is only populated for delta files.

- **lower_bound_tsn**
  This is the timestamp for the earliest transaction covered by this checkpoint file.

- **upper_bound_tsn**
  This is the timestamp for the last transaction covered by this checkpoint file.

- **checkpoint_file_id**
  This is the internal identifier for the file.

- **relative_file_path**
  The location of the file relative to the checkpoint file container.

The metadata of all CFPs that exist on disk is stored in an internal array structure referred to as the **storage array**. It is a fixed-sized array of 8192 entries, where each entry in the array refers to a CFP, and the array provides support for a cumulative size of 256 GB for durable memory-optimized tables in the database. The internal_storage_slot value in the metadata refers to the location of an entry in this array.

As discussed previously, each CFP contains transactions in a particular timestamp range, and the storage array entries are ordered by timestamp, as shown in Figure 6-4.

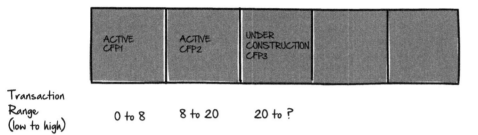

Figure 6-4: The storage array stores metadata for up to 8192 CFPs per database.

The CFPs referenced by the storage array, along with the tail of the log, represent all the on-disk information required to recover the memory-optimized tables in a database.

Let's see an example of some of these checkpoint file state transitions in action. At this stage, our CkptDemo database has one empty table, and we've seen that SQL Server has created 9 CFPs. We'll take a look at the checkpoint file metadata, using the sys. dm_db_xtp_checkpoint_files DMV. In this case, we just return the file type (DATA or DELTA), the state of each file, and the relative path to each file.

```
SELECT  file_type_desc ,
        state_desc ,
        relative_file_path
FROM    sys.dm_db_xtp_checkpoint_files
ORDER BY file_type_desc
GO
```

Listing 6-10: Examine the metadata for your checkpoint files.

Figure 6-5 shows that of the 9 CFPs (9 data files, 9 delta files), 8 CFPs have the state PRECREATED, and the other 1 CFP has the state UNDER CONSTRUCTION.

file_type_desc	state_desc	relative_file_path
DATA	UNDER CONSTRUCTION	84dde134-4b47-4332-a31a-8ac34f8228ac\3122049f-13bb-4c25-a8a5-972980337acc\00000021-00000077-004
DATA	PRECREATED	84dde134-4b47-4332-a31a-8ac34f8228ac\3122049f-13bb-4c25-a8a5-972980337acc\00000021-00000098-00(
DATA	PRECREATED	84dde134-4b47-4332-a31a-8ac34f8228ac\3122049f-13bb-4c25-a8a5-972980337acc\00000021-000000a7-00(
DATA	PRECREATED	84dde134-4b47-4332-a31a-8ac34f8228ac\3122049f-13bb-4c25-a8a5-972980337acc\00000021-000000bf-000
DATA	PRECREATED	84dde134-4b47-4332-a31a-8ac34f8228ac\3122049f-13bb-4c25-a8a5-972980337acc\00000021-000000cb-00(
DATA	PRECREATED	84dde134-4b47-4332-a31a-8ac34f8228ac\3122049f-13bb-4c25-a8a5-972980337acc\00000021-000000ef-000
DATA	PRECREATED	84dde134-4b47-4332-a31a-8ac34f8228ac\3122049f-13bb-4c25-a8a5-972980337acc\00000021-000000b3-00(
DATA	PRECREATED	84dde134-4b47-4332-a31a-8ac34f8228ac\3122049f-13bb-4c25-a8a5-972980337acc\00000021-000000d7-00(
DATA	PRECREATED	84dde134-4b47-4332-a31a-8ac34f8228ac\3122049f-13bb-4c25-a8a5-972980337acc\00000021-000000e3-00(
DELTA	PRECREATED	84dde134-4b47-4332-a31a-8ac34f8228ac\3122049f-13bb-4c25-a8a5-972980337acc\00000021-000000ba-00(
DELTA	PRECREATED	84dde134-4b47-4332-a31a-8ac34f8228ac\3122049f-13bb-4c25-a8a5-972980337acc\00000021-000000f6-000:
DELTA	UNDER CONSTRUCTION	84dde134-4b47-4332-a31a-8ac34f8228ac\3122049f-13bb-4c25-a8a5-972980337acc\00000021-00000093-00(
DELTA	PRECREATED	84dde134-4b47-4332-a31a-8ac34f8228ac\3122049f-13bb-4c25-a8a5-972980337acc\00000021-000000d2-00(
DELTA	PRECREATED	84dde134-4b47-4332-a31a-8ac34f8228ac\3122049f-13bb-4c25-a8a5-972980337acc\00000021-000000a2-00(
DELTA	PRECREATED	84dde134-4b47-4332-a31a-8ac34f8228ac\3122049f-13bb-4c25-a8a5-972980337acc\00000021-000000de-00(
DELTA	PRECREATED	84dde134-4b47-4332-a31a-8ac34f8228ac\3122049f-13bb-4c25-a8a5-972980337acc\00000021-000000ae-00(
DELTA	PRECREATED	84dde134-4b47-4332-a31a-8ac34f8228ac\3122049f-13bb-4c25-a8a5-972980337acc\00000021-000000c6-00(
DELTA	PRECREATED	84dde134-4b47-4332-a31a-8ac34f8228ac\3122049f-13bb-4c25-a8a5-972980337acc\00000021-000000aa-00(

Figure 6-5:   The 16 checkpoint files after creating a memory-optimized table.

The values in the `relative_file_path` column are a concatenation of the two GUID folder names, plus the file names in the folder that was populated when we created the table. These relative paths are of the general form `GUID1\GUID2\FILENAME` where `GUID1` is the GUID for the container, `GUID2` is the GUID for the file in the container and `FILENAME` is the name of the individual data or delta file. For example, the `FILENAME` portion of the relative path for the third row in Figure 6-5 is 00000021–000000a7–0003, which matches the name of the second file (the first data file) listed in my file browser previously, in Figure 6-3.

Let's now put some rows into the t_memopt table, as shown in Listing 6-11. The script also backs up the database so that we can make log backups later (although the backup does not affect what we will shortly see in the metadata).

```
-- INSERT 8000 rows.
-- This should load 5 16MB data files on a machine with <= 16GB of memory.
SET NOCOUNT ON;
DECLARE @i INT = 0
WHILE ( @i < 8000 )
    BEGIN
        INSERT    t_memopt
        VALUES  ( @i, 'a', REPLICATE('b', 8000) )
        SET @i += 1;
    END;
GO
```

```
BACKUP DATABASE [CkptDemo] TO  DISK = N'C:\BackupsHK\CkptDemo_data.bak'
   WITH NOFORMAT, INIT,  NAME = N'CkptDemo-Full Database Backup', SKIP,
        NOREWIND, NOUNLOAD,  STATS = 10;
GO
```

Listing 6-11: Populate the memory-optimized tables with 8000 rows and back up the database.

If we peek again into the GUID-named subfolder in the file system browser, we should see four additional CFPs.

Now let's return to look at the checkpoint file metadata in a little more detail by rerunning the query in Listing 6-9. Figure 6-6 shows the 13 CFPs returned, and the property values for each file.

file_type_desc	state_desc	internal_storage...	file_size_in_bytes	inserted_row_count	deleted_row_count	lower_bound_tsn	upper_bound_tsn
DATA	PRECREATED	NULL	16777216	0	NULL	NULL	NULL
DATA	PRECREATED	NULL	16777216	0	NULL	NULL	NULL
DATA	PRECREATED	NULL	16777216	0	NULL	NULL	NULL
DATA	PRECREATED	NULL	16777216	0	NULL	NULL	NULL
DATA	PRECREATED	NULL	16777216	0	NULL	NULL	NULL
DATA	PRECREATED	NULL	16777216	0	NULL	NULL	NULL
DATA	PRECREATED	NULL	16777216	0	NULL	NULL	NULL
DATA	PRECREATED	NULL	16777216	0	NULL	NULL	NULL
DATA	UNDER CONSTRUCTION	NULL	16777216	496	NULL	7506	NULL
DATA	UNDER CONSTRUCTION	NULL	16777216	1876	NULL	NULL	1878
DATA	UNDER CONSTRUCTION	NULL	16777216	1876	NULL	1878	3754
DATA	UNDER CONSTRUCTION	NULL	16777216	1876	NULL	3754	5630
DATA	UNDER CONSTRUCTION	NULL	16777216	1876	NULL	5630	7506
DELTA	PRECREATED	NULL	1048576	NULL	0	NULL	NULL
DELTA	PRECREATED	NULL	1048576	NULL	0	NULL	NULL
DELTA	PRECREATED	NULL	1048576	NULL	0	NULL	NULL
DELTA	PRECREATED	NULL	1048576	NULL	0	NULL	NULL
DELTA	PRECREATED	NULL	1048576	NULL	0	NULL	NULL
DELTA	PRECREATED	NULL	1048576	NULL	0	NULL	NULL
DELTA	PRECREATED	NULL	1048576	NULL	0	NULL	NULL
DELTA	PRECREATED	NULL	1048576	NULL	0	NULL	NULL
DELTA	UNDER CONSTRUCTION	NULL	1048576	NULL	0	7506	NULL
DELTA	UNDER CONSTRUCTION	NULL	1048576	NULL	0	NULL	1878
DELTA	UNDER CONSTRUCTION	NULL	1048576	NULL	0	1878	3754
DELTA	UNDER CONSTRUCTION	NULL	1048576	NULL	0	3754	5630
DELTA	UNDER CONSTRUCTION	NULL	1048576	NULL	0	5630	7506

Figure 6-6: Contents of the `sys.dm_db_xtp_checkpoint_files` view.

Notice that there are no **ACTIVE** data files because there has been no checkpoint event yet. However, we now have five **UNDER CONSTRUCTION** CFPs and, because of the continuous checkpointing, the data files of these CFPs contain 8000 data rows (four files have 1876 rows and one has 496, as we can see from the `inserted_row_count` column). If SQL Server needed to recover this table's data at this point, it would do it completely from the transaction log.

However, let's see what happens when a checkpoint event occurs, also referred to closing a checkpoint.

Closing a checkpoint

Let's now actually execute the checkpoint command in this database, manually, and then rerun Listing 6-11 to interrogate the metadata in `sys.dm_db_xtp_checkpoint_files`.

```
CHECKPOINT;
GO
-- now rerun Listing 6-11
```

Listing 6-12:   Manual checkpoint in the CkptDemo database.

In the output, we'll see one or more CFPs (in this case, five) with the state **ACTIVE** and with non-**NULL** values for the `internal_storage_slot`, as shown in Figure 6-7.

file_type_desc	state_desc	internal_storage_slot	file_size_in_bytes	inserted_row_count	deleted_row_count	lower_bound_tsn	upper_bound_tsn
DATA	ACTIVE	0	16777216	1876	NULL	NULL	1878
DATA	ACTIVE	1	16777216	1876	NULL	1878	3754
DATA	ACTIVE	2	16777216	1876	NULL	3754	5630
DATA	ACTIVE	3	16777216	1876	NULL	5630	7506
DATA	ACTIVE	4	16777216	496	NULL	7506	8003
DATA	PRECREATED	NULL	16777216	0	NULL	NULL	NULL
DATA	PRECREATED	NULL	16777216	0	NULL	NULL	NULL
DATA	PRECREATED	NULL	16777216	0	NULL	NULL	NULL
DATA	PRECREATED	NULL	16777216	0	NULL	NULL	NULL
DATA	PRECREATED	NULL	16777216	0	NULL	NULL	NULL
DATA	PRECREATED	NULL	16777216	0	NULL	NULL	NULL
DATA	PRECREATED	NULL	16777216	0	NULL	NULL	NULL
DATA	PRECREATED	NULL	16777216	0	NULL	NULL	NULL
DELTA	ACTIVE	0	1048576	NULL	0	NULL	1878
DELTA	ACTIVE	1	1048576	NULL	0	1878	3754
DELTA	ACTIVE	2	1048576	NULL	0	3754	5630
DELTA	ACTIVE	3	1048576	NULL	0	5630	7506
DELTA	ACTIVE	4	1048576	NULL	0	7506	8003
DELTA	PRECREATED	NULL	1048576	NULL	0	NULL	NULL
DELTA	PRECREATED	NULL	1048576	NULL	0	NULL	NULL
DELTA	PRECREATED	NULL	1048576	NULL	0	NULL	NULL
DELTA	PRECREATED	NULL	1048576	NULL	0	NULL	NULL
DELTA	PRECREATED	NULL	1048576	NULL	0	NULL	NULL
DELTA	PRECREATED	NULL	1048576	NULL	0	NULL	NULL
DELTA	PRECREATED	NULL	1048576	NULL	0	NULL	NULL

Figure 6-7:   The CFPs after running the checkpoint command.

Notice that the five **ACTIVE** CFPs have consecutive `internal_storage_slot` values. In fact, if we execute a checkpoint multiple times, we'll see that each checkpoint will create additional **ACTIVE** CFPs, with contiguous values for `internal_storage_slot`.

What's happened here is that the checkpoint event takes a section of the transaction log not covered by a previous checkpoint event, and converts all operations on memory-optimized tables contained in that section of the log into one or more **ACTIVE** CFPs. Once the checkpoint task finishes processing the log, the checkpoint is completed with the following steps:

1.   All buffered writes (all writes that are currently only present in the in-memory table) are flushed to the data and delta files.

143

2. A checkpoint inventory is constructed that includes descriptors for all files from the previous checkpoint plus any files added by the current checkpoint. The inventory is hardened to the transaction log.

3. The location of the inventory is stored in the transaction log so that it is available at recovery time.

With a completed checkpoint (i.e. the **ACTIVE** CFPs that a checkpoint event creates), combined with the tail of the transaction log, SQL Server can recover any memory-optimized table. A checkpoint event has a timestamp, which indicates that the effects of all transactions before the checkpoint timestamp are recorded in files created by the checkpoint and thus the transaction log is not needed to recover them. Of course, just as for disk-based tables, even though that section of the log has been covered by a checkpoint it can still not be truncated till we've had a log backup.

As discussed previously, the **ACTIVE** CFPs created by a checkpoint event are "closed" in the sense that the continuous checkpointing process no longer writes new rows to these data files, but it will still need to write to the associated delta files, to reflect deletion of existing row versions.

Merging checkpoint files

As we've seen, the set of files involved in a checkpoint grows with each checkpoint event. However, the meaningful content of a data file decreases as more and more of its row versions are marked as deleted in the corresponding delta file. Since the recovery process will read the contents of all data and delta files recorded in the checkpoint inventory in the log, performance of crash recovery degrades as the number of relevant rows in each data file decreases.

The solution to this problem is to **merge** data files that are adjacent in terms of timestamp ranges, when their active content (the percentage of undeleted versions in a data file) drops below a threshold. Merging two data files, DF1 and DF2, results in a new data file,

DF3, covering the combined range of DF1 and DF2. All deleted versions identified in the delta files for DF1 and DF2 are removed during the merge. The delta file for DF3 is empty immediately after the merge, except for deletions that occurred after the merge operation started.

Merging can also occur when two adjacent data files are each less than 50% full. Data files can end up only partially full if a manual checkpoint has been run, which closes the currently open (UNDER CONSTRUCTION) checkpoint data file and starts a new one.

Automatic merge

To identify a set of files to be merged, a background task periodically looks at all ACTIVE data/delta file pairs and identifies zero or more sets of files that qualify.

Each set can contain two or more data/delta file pairs that are adjacent to each other such that the resultant set of rows can still fit in a single data file of size 128 MB (or 16 MB for machines with 16 GB memory or less). Table 6-1 shows some examples of files that will be chosen to be merged under the merge policy.

Adjacent source files (%full)	Merge selection
DF0 (30%), DF1 (50%), DF2 (50%), DF3 (90%)	(DF1, DF2)
DF0 (30%), DF1 (20%), DF2 (50%), DF3 (10%)	(DF0, DF1, DF2). Files are chosen starting from left.
DF0 (80%), DF1 (10%), DF2 (10%), DF3 (20%)	(DF0, DF1, DF2). Files are chosen starting from left.

Table 6-1: Examples of files that can be chosen for file merge operations.

It is possible that two adjacent data files are 60% full. They will not be merged and 40% of storage is unused. So the total disk storage used for durable memory-optimized tables is effectively larger than the corresponding memory-optimized size. In the worst case, the size of storage space taken by durable tables could be two times larger than the corresponding memory-optimized size.

Manual merge

In most cases, the automatic merging of checkpoint files will be sufficient to keep the number of files manageable. However, in rare situations or for testing purposes, you might want to use a manual merge. We can use the procedure **sp_xtp_merge_checkpoint_files** to force a manual merge of checkpoint files. To determine which files might be eligible, we can look at the metadata in **sys.dm_db_xtp_checkpoint_files**.

Remember that earlier we turned off automatic merging of files using the undocumented trace flag, 9851. Again, this is *not recommended* in a production system but, for the sake of this example, it does allow us to explore more readily this metadata and how it evolves during a merge operation.

In continuing our previous example, let's now delete half the rows in the **t_memopt** table as shown in Listing 6-13.

```
SET NOCOUNT ON;
DECLARE @i INT = 0;
WHILE ( @i <= 8000 )
    BEGIN
        DELETE   t_memopt
        WHERE    c1 = @i;
        SET @i += 2;
    END;
GO
CHECKPOINT;
GO
```

Listing 6-13:   Delete half the rows in the memory-optimized table.

146

The metadata will now look something like that shown in Figure 6-8, with one additional CFP and with row counts in the deleted_rows column, since the table has only half as many rows.

file_type_desc	state_desc	internal_storage_slot	file_size_in_bytes	inserted_row_count	deleted_row_count	lower_bound_tsn	upper_bound_tsn
DATA	ACTIVE	0	16777216	1876	NULL	NULL	1878
DATA	ACTIVE	1	16777216	1876	NULL	1878	3754
DATA	ACTIVE	2	16777216	1876	NULL	3754	5630
DATA	ACTIVE	3	16777216	1876	NULL	5630	7506
DATA	ACTIVE	4	16777216	496	NULL	7506	8003
DATA	ACTIVE	5	16777216	0	NULL	8003	12007
DATA	PRECREATED	NULL	16777216	0	NULL	NULL	NULL
DATA	PRECREATED	NULL	16777216	0	NULL	NULL	NULL
DATA	PRECREATED	NULL	16777216	0	NULL	NULL	NULL
DATA	PRECREATED	NULL	16777216	0	NULL	NULL	NULL
DATA	PRECREATED	NULL	16777216	0	NULL	NULL	NULL
DATA	PRECREATED	NULL	16777216	0	NULL	NULL	NULL
DATA	PRECREATED	NULL	16777216	0	NULL	NULL	NULL
DELTA	ACTIVE	0	1048576	NULL	938	NULL	1878
DELTA	ACTIVE	1	1048576	NULL	938	1878	3754
DELTA	ACTIVE	2	1048576	NULL	938	3754	5630
DELTA	ACTIVE	3	1048576	NULL	938	5630	7506
DELTA	ACTIVE	4	1048576	NULL	248	7506	8003
DELTA	ACTIVE	5	1048576	NULL	0	8003	12007
DELTA	PRECREATED	NULL	1048576	NULL	0	NULL	NULL
DELTA	PRECREATED	NULL	1048576	NULL	0	NULL	NULL
DELTA	PRECREATED	NULL	1048576	NULL	0	NULL	NULL
DELTA	PRECREATED	NULL	1048576	NULL	0	NULL	NULL
DELTA	PRECREATED	NULL	1048576	NULL	0	NULL	NULL
DELTA	PRECREATED	NULL	1048576	NULL	0	NULL	NULL
DELTA	PRECREATED	NULL	1048576	NULL	0	NULL	NULL
DELTA	PRECREATED	NULL	1048576	NULL	0	NULL	NULL

Figure 6-8: The checkpoint file metadata after deleting half the rows in the table.

The number of deleted rows, spread across five files adds up to 4000, as expected. From this information, we can find adjacent files that are not full, or files that we can see have a lot of their rows removed. Armed with the transaction_id_lower_bound from the first file in the set, and the transaction_id_upper_bound from the last file, we can call the sys.sp_xtp_merge_checkpoint_files procedure, as in Listing 6-14, to force a manual merge. Note that this procedure will not accept a NULL as a parameter, so if the transaction_id_lower_bound is NULL, we can use any value less than transaction_id_upper_bound.

```
EXEC sys.sp_xtp_merge_checkpoint_files 'CkptDemo', 1877, 12007
GO
```

Listing 6-14:   Force a manual merge of checkpoint files.

We can verify the state of the merge operation with another DMV,
`sys.dm_db_xtp_merge_requests`, as shown in Listing 6-15.

```
SELECT   request_state_desc ,
         lower_bound_tsn ,
         upper_bound_tsn
FROM     sys.dm_db_xtp_merge_requests;
GO
```

Listing 6-15:   Verify the state of the merge request.

The output should look similar to Figure 6-9.

request_state_desc	lower_bound_tsn	upper_bound_tsn
PENDING	0	12018

Figure 6-9:   Merge operation is pending.

In the metadata, we should now see one new CFP in the **MERGE TARGET** state containing
all the 4000 remaining rows (from here in, I've filtered out the **PRECREATED** files).

	file_type_desc	state_desc	internal_storage_slot	file_size_in_bytes	inserted_row_count	deleted_row_count	lower_bound_tsn	upper_bound_tsn
1	DATA	ACTIVE	0	16777216	1876	NULL	NULL	1878
2	DATA	ACTIVE	1	16777216	1876	NULL	1878	3754
3	DATA	ACTIVE	2	16777216	1876	NULL	3754	5630
4	DATA	ACTIVE	3	16777216	1876	NULL	5630	7506
5	DATA	ACTIVE	4	16777216	496	NULL	7506	8003
6	DATA	ACTIVE	5	16777216	0	NULL	8003	12007
7	DATA	MERGE TARGET	NULL	33554432	4000	NULL	NULL	NULL
8	DELTA	ACTIVE	0	1048576	NULL	938	NULL	1878
9	DELTA	ACTIVE	1	1048576	NULL	938	1878	3754
10	DELTA	ACTIVE	2	1048576	NULL	938	3754	5630
11	DELTA	ACTIVE	3	1048576	NULL	938	5630	7506
12	DELTA	ACTIVE	4	1048576	NULL	248	7506	8003
13	DELTA	ACTIVE	5	1048576	NULL	0	8003	12007
14	DELTA	MERGE TARGET	NULL	1048576	NULL	0	NULL	NULL

Figure 6-10: Some of the checkpoint file metadata after a requested merge.

Now run another manual checkpoint and then, once the merge is complete, the `request_state_description` column of `sys.dm_db_xtp_merge_requests` should show a value of `INSTALLED` instead of `PENDING`. The metadata will now look similar to Figure 6-11. Now the CFP in slot 5, containing the 4000 remaining rows, is `ACTIVE` and once again the checkpoint creates a new `ACTIVE` CFP (slot 6). The original 6 CFPs (originally slots 0–5) have been merged and their status is `MERGED SOURCE`. If any concurrent activity were occurring on the server, we'd also see new `UNDER CONSTRUCTION` CFPs.

	file_type_desc	state_desc	internal_storage_slot	file_size_in_bytes	inserted_row_count	deleted_row_count	lower_bound_tsn	upper_bound_tsn
1	DATA	ACTIVE	5	33554432	4000	NULL	NULL	12007
2	DATA	ACTIVE	6	16777216	0	NULL	12007	12013
3	DATA	MERGED SOURCE	NULL	16777216	1876	NULL	NULL	1878
4	DATA	MERGED SOURCE	NULL	16777216	1876	NULL	1878	3754
5	DATA	MERGED SOURCE	NULL	16777216	1876	NULL	3754	5630
6	DATA	MERGED SOURCE	NULL	16777216	1876	NULL	5630	7506
7	DATA	MERGED SOURCE	NULL	16777216	496	NULL	7506	8003
8	DATA	MERGED SOURCE	NULL	16777216	0	NULL	8003	12007
9	DELTA	ACTIVE	5	1048576	NULL	0	NULL	12007
10	DELTA	ACTIVE	6	1048576	NULL	0	12007	12013
11	DELTA	MERGED SOURCE	NULL	1048576	NULL	938	NULL	1878
12	DELTA	MERGED SOURCE	NULL	1048576	NULL	938	1878	3754
13	DELTA	MERGED SOURCE	NULL	1048576	NULL	938	3754	5630
14	DELTA	MERGED SOURCE	NULL	1048576	NULL	938	5630	7506
15	DELTA	MERGED SOURCE	NULL	1048576	NULL	248	7506	8003
16	DELTA	MERGED SOURCE	NULL	1048576	NULL	0	8003	12007

Figure 6-11: The checkpoint file metadata after forcing a merge operation.

Note that the six CFPs that are included in the merged transaction range are still visible, but they have no `internal_storage_slot` number, which means they are no longer used for any ongoing operations. We see an ACTIVE data file containing all 4000 rows in it and includes the complete transaction range.

Finally, remember to turn off Trace Flag 9851.

```
DBCC TRACEOFF (9851, -1);
```

Listing 6-16: Disable Trace Flag 9851.

Garbage collection of checkpoint files

Once the merge operation is complete, the checkpoint files with a state of MERGED SOURCE are not needed and can be removed by the garbage collection process at a later time, as long as regular log backups are taken.

A file needs to go through three stages before it is actually removed by the garbage collection process. Let us assume we are merging files A (data/delta), B (data/delta) into C (data/delta). Following are the key steps.

Stage 1: Checkpoint

After the merge has completed, the in-memory engine cannot remove the original MERGED SOURCE files (A and B) until a checkpoint event occurs that guarantees that data in those files is no longer needed for recovery, in the event of a service interruption (of course, they certainly will be required for restore and recovery after a disk failure, so we need to be running backups).

The checkpoint directly after the forced merge produced the MERGED SOURCE CFPs, and running another one now sees them transition to REQUIRED FOR BACKUP/HA.

	file_type_desc	state_desc	internal_storage_slot	file_size_in_bytes	inserted_row_count	deleted_row_count	lower_bound_tsn	upper_bou
1	DATA	ACTIVE	5	33554432	4000	NULL	NULL	12007
2	DATA	ACTIVE	7	16777216	0	NULL	12007	12034
3	DATA	MERGED SOURCE	NULL	16777216	0	NULL	12007	12013
4	DATA	MERGED SOURCE	NULL	16777216	0	NULL	12013	12034
5	DATA	REQUIRED FOR BACKUP/HA	NULL	NULL	NULL	NULL	NULL	NULL
6	DATA	REQUIRED FOR BACKUP/HA	NULL	NULL	NULL	NULL	NULL	NULL
7	DATA	REQUIRED FOR BACKUP/HA	NULL	NULL	NULL	NULL	NULL	NULL
8	DATA	REQUIRED FOR BACKUP/HA	NULL	NULL	NULL	NULL	NULL	NULL
9	DATA	REQUIRED FOR BACKUP/HA	NULL	NULL	NULL	NULL	NULL	NULL
10	DATA	REQUIRED FOR BACKUP/HA	NULL	NULL	NULL	NULL	NULL	NULL
11	DELTA	ACTIVE	5	1048576	NULL	0	NULL	12007
12	DELTA	ACTIVE	7	1048576	NULL	0	12007	12034
13	DELTA	MERGED SOURCE	NULL	1048576	NULL	0	12007	12013
14	DELTA	MERGED SOURCE	NULL	1048576	NULL	0	12013	12034
15	DELTA	REQUIRED FOR BACKUP/HA	NULL	NULL	NULL	NULL	NULL	NULL
16	DELTA	REQUIRED FOR BACKUP/HA	NULL	NULL	NULL	NULL	NULL	NULL
17	DELTA	REQUIRED FOR BACKUP/HA	NULL	NULL	NULL	NULL	NULL	NULL

Figure 6-12: The checkpoint file metadata a merge, then another checkpoint.

Stage 2: Log backup

SQL Server needs to guarantee via a log backup that the log truncation point has moved safely to a point beyond where the CFP files will be required (for databases using the SIMPLE recovery model, log backups are not required).

```
BACKUP LOG [CkptDemo] TO  DISK = N'C:\BackupsHK\CkptDemo_log.bak'
    WITH NOFORMAT, INIT,  NAME = N'CkptDemo-LOG Backup';
```

Listing 6-17: Backing up the log.

Having performed a log backup, SQL Server can mark the source files from the merge operation with the LSN, and any files with an LSN lower than the log truncation point are eligible for garbage collection. Normally, of course, the whole garbage collection process

is automatic, and does not require any intervention, but for our example we can force
the process manually using the sp_xtp_checkpoint_force_garbage_collection
system stored procedure, followed by another checkpoint. You may need to run
Listing 6-18 at least twice.

```
EXEC sp_xtp_checkpoint_force_garbage_collection;
GO

CHECKPOINT
GO
```

Listing 6-18:   Forcing checkpoint files into the TOMBSTONE state.

After this stage, the files may or may not still be visible to your in-memory database
engine through the sys.dm_db_xtp_checkpoint_files DMV, but they will be visible
on disk. In my example, I was still able to see the files, with the TOMBSTONE state, but at
some point they will become invisible to this DMV.

	file_type_desc	state_desc	internal_storage_slot	file_size_in_bytes	inserted_row_count	deleted_row_count	lower_bound_tsn	upper_bound_tsn	checkpoint_file_id
1	NULL	TOMBSTONE	NULL	NULL	NULL	NULL	NULL	NULL	NULL
2	NULL	TOMBSTONE	NULL	NULL	NULL	NULL	NULL	NULL	NULL
3	NULL	TOMBSTONE	NULL	NULL	NULL	NULL	NULL	NULL	NULL
4	NULL	TOMBSTONE	NULL	NULL	NULL	NULL	NULL	NULL	NULL
5	NULL	TOMBSTONE	NULL	NULL	NULL	NULL	NULL	NULL	NULL
6	NULL	TOMBSTONE	NULL	NULL	NULL	NULL	NULL	NULL	NULL
7	NULL	TOMBSTONE	NULL	NULL	NULL	NULL	NULL	NULL	NULL
8	NULL	TOMBSTONE	NULL	NULL	NULL	NULL	NULL	NULL	NULL
9	NULL	TOMBSTONE	NULL	NULL	NULL	NULL	NULL	NULL	NULL
10	NULL	TOMBSTONE	NULL	NULL	NULL	NULL	NULL	NULL	NULL
11	NULL	TOMBSTONE	NULL	NULL	NULL	NULL	NULL	NULL	NULL
12	NULL	TOMBSTONE	NULL	NULL	NULL	NULL	NULL	NULL	NULL
13	NULL	TOMBSTONE	NULL	NULL	NULL	NULL	NULL	NULL	NULL
14	NULL	TOMBSTONE	NULL	NULL	NULL	NULL	NULL	NULL	NULL
15	NULL	TOMBSTONE	NULL	NULL	NULL	NULL	NULL	NULL	NULL
16	NULL	TOMBSTONE	NULL	NULL	NULL	NULL	NULL	NULL	NULL
17	DATA	ACTIVE	8	33554432	4000	NULL	NULL	12007	F7655388-D2E0-4

Figure 6-13:   TOMBSTONE state files in the metadata.

Before a CFP can be removed, the in-memory OLTP engine must ensure that it will not be required. In general, the garbage collection process is automatic. However, there is an option to force the garbage collection of unused checkpoint files.

Stage 3: Unused files garbage collected

Now files A and B can be removed by the system garbage collection process, using the same mechanism as for regular `filestream` files. As for Stage 2, this requires running a set of steps at least twice. The code is in Listing 6-19.

```
BACKUP LOG [CkptDemo] TO  DISK = N'C:\BackupsHK\CkptDemo_log.bak'
    WITH NOFORMAT, INIT,  NAME = N'CkptDemo-LOG Backup';
GO
EXEC sp_filestream_force_garbage_collection;
GO
```

Listing 6-19:   Forcing checkpoint files to be removed from disk.

After Stage 3, the files may no longer be visible through the operating system although, depending on what else is happening on the system, this process may take a while. Keep in mind, however, that normally performing any of this manual garbage collection process should not be necessary.

If you find you do need to implement this manual garbage collection of files, be sure to account for these extra transaction log backups that were performed. You will need to make sure any third-party backup solutions are aware of these log backup files. Alternatively, you could perform a full database backup after performing this manual garbage collection, so that subsequent transaction log backups would use that as their starting point.

Recovery

Recovery on in-memory OLTP tables starts after the location of the most recent checkpoint inventory has been recovered during a scan of the tail of the log. Once the SQL Server host has communicated the location of the checkpoint inventory to the in-memory OLTP engine, SQL Server and in-memory OLTP recovery proceed in parallel. The global transaction timestamp is initialized during the recovery process with the highest transaction timestamp found among the transactions recovered.

In-memory OLTP recovery itself is parallelized. Each delta file represents a filter to eliminate rows that don't have to be loaded from the corresponding data file. This data/delta file pair arrangement means that checkpoint file loading can proceed in parallel across multiple I/O streams with each stream processing a single data file and delta file. The in-memory OLTP engine creates one thread per core to handle parallel insertion of the data produced by the I/O streams. The insert threads load into memory all active rows in the data file after removing the rows that have been deleted. Using one thread per core means that the load process is performed as efficiently as possible.

As the data rows are loaded they are linked into each index defined on the table the row belongs to. For each hash index, the row is added to the chain for the appropriate hash bucket. For each range index, the row is added to the chain for the row's key value, or a new index entry is created if the key value doesn't duplicate one already encountered during recovery of the table.

Finally, once the checkpoint file load process completes, the tail of the transaction log is replayed from the timestamp of the last checkpoint, with the goal of bringing the database back to the state that existed at the time of the crash.

Summary

In this chapter we looked at how the logging process for memory-optimized tables is more efficient than that for disk-based tables, providing additional performance improvement for your in-memory operations. We also looked at how your data changes are persisted to disk using streaming checkpoint files, so that your data is persisted and can be recovered when the SQL Server service is restarted, or your databases containing memory-optimized tables are restored.

Additional Resources

- **A white paper describing FILESTREAM storage and management**:
  HTTP://TINYURL.COM/KZZ37F9.

- **Durability for memory-optimized tables**:
  HTTP://TINYURL.COM/KS4LXD4.

- **State transitions during merging of checkpoint files**:
  HTTP://TINYURL.COM/MGMRPFR.

Chapter 7: Native Compilation of Tables and Stored Procedures

In-memory OLTP introduces the concept of native compilation into SQL Server 2014. In this version, SQL Server can natively compile stored procedures that access memory-optimized tables and, in fact, memory-optimized tables themselves are natively compiled. In many cases, native compilation allows faster data access and more efficient query execution than traditional interpreted T-SQL.

The performance benefit of using a natively compiled stored procedure increases with the number of rows and the complexity of the procedure's code. If a procedure needs to process just a single row, it's unlikely to benefit from native compilation, but it will almost certainly exhibit better performance, compared to interpreted procedure, if it uses one or more of the following:

- aggregation
- nested-loops joins
- multi-statement `SELECT`, `INSERT`, `UPDATE`, and `DELETE` operations
- complex expressions
- procedural logic, such as conditional statements and loops.

You should consider using natively compiled stored procedures for the most performance-critical parts of your applications, including procedures that you execute frequently, that contain logic such as that described above, and that need to be extremely fast.

What Is Native Compilation?

Native compilation refers to the process of converting programming constructs to native code, consisting of processor instructions that can be executed directly by the CPU, without the need for further compilation or interpretation.

The T-SQL language consists of high-level constructs such as CREATE TABLE and SELECT...FROM. The in-memory OLTP compiler takes these constructs, and compiles them down to native code for fast runtime data access and query execution. The in-memory OLTP compiler in SQL Server 2014 takes the table and stored procedures definitions as input. It generates C code, and leverages the Visual C compiler to generate the native code. The result of the compilation of tables and stored procedures is DLLs that are loaded into memory and linked into the SQL Server process.

SQL Server compiles both memory-optimized tables and natively compiled stored procedures to native DLLs at the time of creation. Following a SQL Server instance restart or a failover, table and stored procedure DLLs are recompiled on first access or execution. The information necessary to recreate the DLLs is stored in the database metadata; the DLLs themselves are not part of the database and are not included as part of database backups.

Maintenance of DLLs

The DLLs for memory-optimized tables and natively compiled stored procedures are stored in the file system, along with other generated files, which are kept for trouble-shooting and supportability purposes.

The query in Listing 7-1 shows all table and stored procedure DLLs currently loaded in memory on the server.

```
SELECT   name ,
         description
FROM     sys.dm_os_loaded_modules
WHERE    description = 'XTP Native DLL'
```

Listing 7-1:   Display the list of all table and procedure DLLs currently loaded.

Database administrators do not need to maintain the files that native compilation generates. SQL Server automatically removes generated files that are no longer needed, for example on table and stored procedure deletion and on dropping a database, but also on server or database restart.

Native Compilation of Tables

Creating a memory-optimized table using the **CREATE TABLE** statement results, not only in the table and index structures being created in memory, but also in the table definition being written to the database metadata, and the table being compiled into a DLL.

Consider the script in Listing 7-2, which creates a database and a single, memory-optimized table, and then retrieves the path of the DLL for the table, from the **sys. dm_os_loaded_modules** DMV.

```
USE master
GO
CREATE DATABASE NativeCompDemo ON
    PRIMARY (NAME = NativeCompDemo_Data,
             FILENAME = 'c:\DataHK\NativeCompDemo_Data.mdf',
             SIZE=500MB)
    LOG ON (NAME = NativeCompDemo_log,
             FILENAME = 'c:\DataHK\NativeCompDemo_log.ldf',
             SIZE=500MB);
GO
```

```
ALTER DATABASE NativeCompDemo
    ADD FILEGROUP NativeCompDemo_mod_fg
          CONTAINS MEMORY_OPTIMIZED_DATA
GO
-- adjust filename and path as needed
ALTER DATABASE NativeCompDemo
   ADD FILE (name='NativeCompDemo_mod_dir',
              filename='c:\DataHK\NativeCompDemo_mod_dir')
TO FILEGROUP NativeCompDemo_mod_fg
GO

USE NativeCompDemo
GO
CREATE TABLE dbo.t1
    (
       c1 INT NOT NULL
            PRIMARY KEY NONCLUSTERED ,
       c2 INT
    )
WITH (MEMORY_OPTIMIZED=ON)
GO

-- retrieve the path of the DLL for table t1
SELECT   name ,
         description
FROM     sys.dm_os_loaded_modules
WHERE    name LIKE '%xtp_t_' + CAST(DB_ID() AS VARCHAR(10)) + '_'
         + CAST(OBJECT_ID('dbo.t1') AS VARCHAR(10)) + '.dll'
GO
```

Listing 7-2:   Create a new data and memory-optimized table.

The table creation results in the compilation of the table DLL, and also loading that DLL in memory. The DMV query immediately after the **CREATE TABLE** statement retrieves the path of the table DLL. My results are shown in Figure 7-1.

name	description
C:\Program Files\Microsoft SQL Server\MSSQL12.MSSQLSERVER\MSSQL\DATA\xtp\8\xtp_t_8_277576027.dll	XTP Native DLL

Figure 7-1:   The file path of the DLL for my table.

The table DLL for t1 understands the index structures and row format of the table. SQL Server uses the DLL for traversing indexes and retrieving rows, as well as for determining the data contents of the rows.

Native Compilation of Stored Procedures

The in-memory OLTP engine will natively compile any stored procedure that includes the clause WITH NATIVE_COMPILATION. This means the T-SQL statements in the procedure are all compiled to native code, for efficient execution.

Consider the stored procedure in Listing 7-3, which inserts a million rows into the table t1 from Listing 7-2.

```
CREATE PROCEDURE dbo.p1
WITH NATIVE_COMPILATION, SCHEMABINDING, EXECUTE AS OWNER
AS
BEGIN ATOMIC
WITH (TRANSACTION ISOLATION LEVEL=snapshot, LANGUAGE=N'us_english')
  DECLARE @i INT = 1000000
  WHILE @i > 0
    BEGIN
        INSERT  dbo.t1
        VALUES  ( @i, @i + 1 )
        SET @i -= 1
    END
END
GO
EXEC dbo.p1
GO
```

Listing 7-3:   Creating a natively compiled procedure.

Two other requirements when creating a natively compiled stored procedure are as follows:

- Use of **WITH SCHEMABINDING** – guarantees that the tables accessed by the procedure are not dropped. Normally, schemabinding also prevents the underlying objects from being altered, but since memory-optimized tables cannot ever be altered, that restriction is irrelevant for natively compiled procedures.

- Use of **BEGIN ATOMIC** – natively compiled procedures must start by defining an ATOMIC block. This is an ANSI construct that SQL Server allows only inside natively compiled procedures. An ATOMIC block guarantees that the enclosed operations are processed within a transaction. It starts a transaction if one is not open, and otherwise it creates a SAVEPOINT.

The DLL for the procedure p1 can interact directly with the DLL for the table t1, as well as the in-memory OLTP storage engine, to insert the rows very quickly.

The in-memory OLTP compiler leverages the query optimizer to create an efficient execution plan for each of the queries in the stored procedure. Note that, for natively compiled stored procedures, the query execution plan is compiled into the DLL.

SQL Server 2014 does not support automatic recompilation of natively compiled stored procedures, so if we make changes to table data, we may need to drop and recreate certain procedures to allow incorporation of new query plans into the stored procedure DLLs. SQL Server recompiles natively compiled stored procedures on first execution, after server restart, as well as after failover to an AlwaysOn secondary, meaning that the query optimizer will create new query plans that are subsequently compiled into the stored procedure DLLs.

As discussed in Chapter 2, there are limitations on the T-SQL constructs that can be included in a natively compiled procedure. Natively compiled stored procedures are intended for short, basic OLTP operations, so many of the complex query constructs provided in the language are not allowed. In fact, there are so many restrictions, that the documentation lists the features that are supported, rather than those that are not. You can find the list at this link: HTTP://TINYURL.COM/JVQTGZF.

Parameter Sniffing

Interpreted T-SQL stored procedures are compiled into intermediate physical execution plans at first execution (invocation) time, in contrast to natively compiled stored procedures, which are natively compiled at creation time. When interpreted stored procedures are compiled at invocation, the values of the parameters supplied for this invocation are used by the optimizer when generating the execution plan. This use of parameters during compilation is called parameter sniffing.

SQL Server does not use parameter sniffing for compiling natively compiled stored procedures. All parameters to the stored procedure are considered to have UNKNOWN values.

Compilation and Query Processing

Figure 7-2 illustrates the compilation process for natively compiled stored procedures.

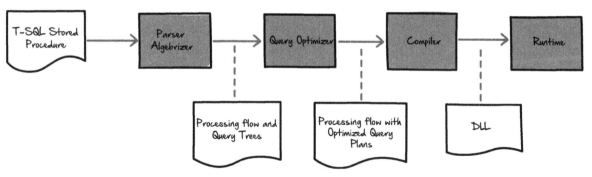

Figure 7-2: Native compilation of stored procedures.

The compilation process is as follows:

1. The user issues a **CREATE PROCEDURE** statement to SQL Server.

2. The parser and algebrizer create the processing flow for the procedure, as well as query trees for the T-SQL queries in the stored procedure.

3. The optimizer creates optimized query execution plans for all the queries in the stored procedure.

4. The in-memory OLTP compiler takes the processing flow with the embedded optimized query plans and generates a DLL that contains the machine code for executing the stored procedure.

5. The generated DLL is loaded in memory and linked to the SQL Server process.

Invocation of a natively compiled stored procedure translates to calling a function in the DLL, as shown in Figure 7-3.

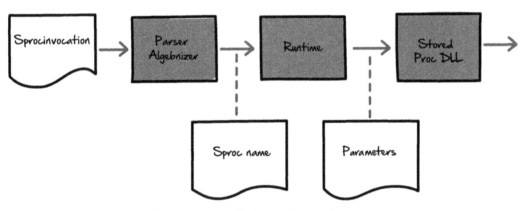

Figure 7-3:   Execution of natively compiled stored procedures.

Execution of natively compiled stored procedures is as follows:

1. The user issues an `'EXEC myproc'` statement.

2. The parser extracts the name and stored procedure parameters.

3. The in-memory OLTP runtime locates the DLL entry point for the stored procedure.

4. The DLL executes the procedure logic and returns the results to the client.

Optimization of Natively Compiled Procedures

Optimization of natively compiled stored procedures has most of the same goals as optimization of interpreted procedures. That is, the optimizer needs to find query plans for each of the statements in the procedure so that those statements can be executed as efficiently as possible. The optimizer is aware that the surface area of allowed T-SQL constructs is limited in natively compiled procedures, so certain transformations it might perform are not supported.

The formula that the optimizer uses for assessing the relative cost of operations on memory-optimized tables is similar to the costing formula for operations on disk-based tables, with only a few exceptions. However, because of differences in the way that memory-optimized tables are organized and managed, the optimizer does need to be aware of different choices it may need to make, and certain execution plan options that are not available when working with memory-optimized tables. The following subsections describe the most important differences between optimizing queries on disk-based tables and optimizing queries on memory-optimized tables.

Index access paths

There are certain limitations to the access paths available to the in-memory engine during query optimization, with respect to its use of hash and range indexes, which I'll summarize briefly.

If the optimizer finds no index that it can use efficiently, it will choose a plan that will effectively be a table scan, although there is really no concept of a table scan with memory-optimized tables, because all data access is through indexes. The compiled plan will indicate that one of the indexes is to be used, through which all of the rows will be retrieved.

Note that for an interop plan, as opposed to a plan for a natively compiled procedure, you may actually see a table scan in the estimated plan. With such a plan, the decision as to which index to use to access all the rows is made by the execution engine at runtime. The usual choice is the hash index with the fewest number of buckets, but that is not guaranteed.

In general, the optimizer will choose to use a hash index over a range index if the cost estimations are the same.

Hash indexes

There are no ordered scans with hash indexes. If a query is looking for a range of values, or requires that the results be returned in sorted order, a hash index will not be useful, and the optimizer will not consider it.

The optimizer cannot use a hash index unless the query filters on all columns in the index key. The hash index examples in Chapter 4 illustrated an index on just a single column. However, just like indexes on disk-based tables, hash indexes on memory-optimized tables can be composite, but the hash function used to determine to which bucket a row belongs is based on all columns in the index. So if we had a hash index on (city, state), a row for a customer from **Springfield, Illinois** would hash to a completely different value than a row for a customer from **Springfield, Missouri**, and also would hash to a completely different value than a row for a customer from **Chicago, Illinois**. If a query only supplies a value for city, a hash value cannot be generated and the index cannot be used, unless the entire index is used for a scan.

For similar reasons, a hash index can only be used if the filter is based on an equality. If the query does not specify an exact value for one of the columns in the hash index key, the hash value cannot be determined. So, if we have a hash index on city, and the query is looking for city LIKE 'San%', a hash lookup is not possible.

Range indexes

Range indexes cannot be scanned in reverse order. There is no concept of "previous pointers" in a range index on a memory-optimized table. With on-disk indexes, if a query requests the data to be sorted in DESC order, the on-disk index could be scanned in reverse order to support this. With in-memory tables, an index would have to be created as a descending index. In fact, it is possible to have two indexes on the same column, one defined as ascending and one defined as descending. It is also possible to have both a range and a hash index on the same column.

No Halloween protection

Halloween protection is not incorporated into the query plans. Halloween protection provides guarantees against accessing the same row multiple times during query processing. Operations on disk-based tables use spooling operators to make sure rows are not accessed repeatedly, but this is not necessary for plans on memory-optimized tables.

The storage engine provides Halloween protection for memory-optimized tables by including a statement ID as part of the row header. Since the statement ID that introduced a row version is stored with the row, if the same statement encounters that row again, it knows it has already been processed.

No parallel plans

Currently, parallel plans are not produced for operations on memory-optimized tables. The XML plan for the query will indicate that the reason for no parallelism is because the table is a memory-optimized table.

No auto-update of statistics

SQL Server In-Memory OLTP does not keep any row modification counters, and does not automatically update statistics on memory-optimized tables. One of the reasons for not updating the statistics is so there will be no chance of dependency failures due to waiting for statistics to be gathered.

You'll need to make sure you set up a process for regularly updating statistics on memory-optimized tables using the UPDATE STATISTICS command, which can be used to update statistics on just one index, or on all the indexes of a specified table. Alternatively, you can use the procedure sp_updatestats, which updates all the statistics on all indexes in a database. For disk-based tables, this procedure only updates statistics on tables which have been modified since the last time statistics were updated, but for memory-optimized tables, the procedure will also recreate statistics. Make sure you have loaded data and updated statistics on all tables accessed in a natively compiled procedure before the procedure is created, since the plan is created at the time of procedure creation, and it will be based on the existing statistics.

Natively compiled procedure plans will never be recompiled on the fly; the only way to get a new plan is to drop and recreate the procedure (or restart the server).

Performance Comparisons

Since the very first versions of SQL Server, stored procedures have been described as being stored in a compiled form. The process of coming up with a query plan for a batch is also frequently described as compilation. However, until SQL Server 2014 and in-memory OLTP, what was described as compilation wasn't really true compilation. SQL Server stored query plans in an internal form, after they had been parsed and normalized, but they were not truly compiled. When executing the plan, the execution engine walks the query tree and interprets each operator as it is executed, calling appropriate database functions. This is far more expensive than for a true compiled plan, composed of machine language calls to actual CPU instructions.

When processing a query, the runtime costs include locking, latching, and disk I/O, and the relatively small cost and overhead associated with interpreted code, compared to compiled code, gets "lost in the noise." However, in true performance tuning methodology, there is always a bottleneck; once we remove one, another becomes apparent. Once we remove the overhead of locking, latching, and disk I/O, the cost of interpreted code becomes a major component, and a potential bottleneck.

The only way to substantially speed up processing time is to reduce the number of internal CPU instructions executed. Assume that in our system we use one million CPU instructions per transaction which results in 100 transactions per second (TPS). To achieve a 10-times performance improvement, to 1,000 TPS, we would have to decrease the number of instructions per second to 100,000, which is a 90% reduction.

To satisfy the original vision for Hekaton, and achieve a 100-times performance improvement, to 10,000 TPS, would mean reducing the number of instructions per second to 10,000, or a 99% reduction! A reduction of this magnitude would be impossible with SQL Server's existing interpretive query engine or any other existing interpretive engine.

With natively compiled code, SQL Server In-Memory OLTP has reduced the number of instructions per second by well over 90%, achieving in some cases an improvement in performance of 30 times or more.

Performance data from Microsoft

Tables 7-1, 7-2, and 7-3 show some performance numbers collected during the in-memory OLTP development process at Microsoft, in October 2013. Both tables reference SQL Server tables with 10,000,000 rows and natively compiled procedures running on an Intel Xeon W3520 processor with a clock speed of 2.67 GHz. They are not intended to be guarantees of the performance benefits you might attain. Just consider them to be an example of what is possible.

Table 7-1 shows the number of CPU cycles needed to SELECT a number of random rows in a single transaction, and the final column shows the percentage improvement for the memory-optimized table.

Transaction size in number of rows read	CPU cycles (in millions)		Improvement
	Disk-based table	Memory-optimized table	
1	0.734	0.040	10.8 times
10	0.937	0.051	18.4 times
100	2.72	0.150	18.1 times
1,000	20.1	1.063	18.9 times
10,000	201	9.85	20.4 times

Table 7-1 Comparing SELECT performance.

The more rows are read, the greater the performance benefit until, by reading 10,000 rows in a transaction, the improvement is greater than 20%.

Table 7-2 shows the number of CPU cycles needed to UPDATE a number of random rows in the same 10,000,000 table with one hash index. Log I/O was disabled for this test, by creating memory-optimized tables using the property SCHEMA_ONLY.

Transaction size in number of rows updated	CPU cycles (in millions)		Improvement
	Disk-based table	Memory-optimized table	
1	0.910	0.045	20.2 times
10	1.38	0.059	23.4 times
100	8.17	0.260	31.4 times
1,000	41.9	1.50	27.9 times
10,000	439	14.4	30.5 times

Table 7-2   Comparing UPDATE performance.

Again, the more rows being processed, the greater the performance benefit when using memory-optimized tables. For UPDATE operations, Microsoft was able to realize a 30-fold gain with 10,000 operations, achieving a throughput of 1.9 million updates per core.

Finally, Table 7-3 gives some performance comparisons for a mixed environment, with both SELECT and UPDATE operations. The workload consists of 50% INSERT transactions that append a batch of 100 rows in each transaction, and 50% SELECT transactions that read the more recently inserted batch of rows.

Table 7-3 shows how many TPS are achieved using first, a disk-based table, second, a memory-optimized table being accessed through interop code, and finally, a memory-optimized table being accessed through a natively compiled procedure.

# of CPUs	Disk-based table	Memory-optimized table accessed using interop	Memory-optimized table accessed using natively compiled procedure
1	985	1,450	4,493
4	2,157	3,066	15,127
8	4,211	6,195	30,589
12	5,834	8,679	37,249

Table 7-3:   TPS increase with memory-optimized tables.

With one CPU, using a natively compiled procedure increased the TPS by more than four times, and for 12 CPUs, the increase was over six times.

Comparing performance for multi-row inserts

For our own testing, we could start with code similar to the script shown in Listing 7-4. It creates a new database called xtp_demo. You may need to adjust the file paths, or you could also use any database with a MEMORY_OPTIMIZED filegroup that you have already created.

After creating the database, the script creates a memory-optimized table called bigtable_inmem. This is a SCHEMA_ONLY memory-optimized table so SQL Server will log the table creation, but will not log any DML on the table, so the data will not be durable.

```
USE master;
GO


IF DB_ID('xtp_demo') IS NOT NULL
 DROP DATABASE xtp_demo;
GO
CREATE DATABASE xtp_demo ON
        PRIMARY
                ( NAME = N'xtp_demo_Data',
                  FILENAME = N'c:\DataHK\xtp_demo_Data.mdf'
                  ),
        FILEGROUP [xtp_demo_mod]
                CONTAINS MEMORY_OPTIMIZED_DATA
                        ( NAME = N'xtp_demo1_mod',
                          FILENAME = N'c:\DataHK\xtp_demo1_mod' ,
                          MAXSIZE = 2GB),
                        ( NAME = N'xtp_demo2_mod',
                          FILENAME = N'd:\DataHK\xtp_demo2_mod' ,
                          MAXSIZE = 2GB)
        LOG ON
                ( NAME = N'xtp_demo_Log',
                  FILENAME = N'c:\DataHK\xtp_demo_log.ldf'
                  );
GO


USE xtp_demo;
GO


------- Create the table -------
CREATE TABLE bigtable_inmem (
        id        uniqueidentifier not null
                constraint pk_biggerbigtable_inmem primary key nonclustered
                        hash with( bucket_count = 2097152 ),

        account_id              int not null,
        trans_type_id smallint not null,
        shop_id                 int not null,
        trans_made              datetime not null,
        trans_amount  decimal( 20, 2 ) not null,
        entry_date              datetime2 not null default( current_timestamp ),
```

```
          --index range_trans_type nonclustered
          -- ( shop_id, trans_type_id, trans_made ),
          --index range_trans_made nonclustered
          --  ( trans_made, shop_id, account_id ),
          index hash_trans_type nonclustered hash
               ( shop_id, trans_type_id, trans_made )
                  with( bucket_count = 2097152),
          index hash_trans_made nonclustered hash
               ( trans_made, shop_id, account_id )
                  with( bucket_count = 2097152)


          )  WITH ( MEMORY_OPTIMIZED=ON,
                        DURABILITY=SCHEMA_ONLY );
GO
```

Listing 7-4:   Creating the `xtp_demo` database, and a `SCHEMA_ONLY` memory-optimized table.

Next, Listing 7-5 creates an interop (not natively compiled) stored procedure called `ins_bigtable` that inserts rows into `bigtable_inmem`. The number of rows to insert is passed as a parameter when the procedure is called.

```
------- Create the procedure -------

CREATE PROC ins_bigtable ( @rows_to_INSERT int )
AS
BEGIN
     SET nocount on;

     DECLARE @i int = 1;
     DECLARE @newid uniqueidentifier
     WHILE @i <= @rows_to_INSERT
     BEGIN
        SET @newid = newid()
        INSERT dbo.bigtable_inmem ( id, account_id, trans_type_id,
                             shop_id, trans_made, trans_amount )
           VALUES( @newid,
               32767 * rand(),
               30 * rand(),
               100 * rand(),
```

```
                   dateadd( second, @i, cast( '20130410' AS datetime ) ),
                       ( 32767 * rand() ) / 100. ) ;

            SET @i = @i + 1;

        END
 END
 GO
```

Listing 7-5:   An interop procedure, `ins_bigtable`, to insert rows into the table.

Finally, Listing 7-6 creates the equivalent natively compiled stored procedure.

```
CREATE PROC ins_native_bigtable ( @rows_to_INSERT int )
      with native_compilation, schemabinding, execute AS owner
 AS
BEGIN ATOMIC WITH
  ( TRANSACTION ISOLATION LEVEL = SNAPSHOT,
    LANGUAGE = N'us_english')
        DECLARE @i int = 1;
        DECLARE @newid uniqueidentifier
        WHILE @i <= @rows_to_INSERT
        BEGIN
           SET @newid = newid()
           INSERT dbo.bigtable_inmem ( id, account_id, trans_type_id,
                               shop_id, trans_made, trans_amount )
              VALUES( @newid,
                  32767 * rand(),
                    30 * rand(),
                   100 * rand(),
                    dateadd( second, @i, cast( '20130410' AS datetime ) ),
                      ( 32767 * rand() ) / 100. ) ;
                SET @i = @i + 1;
        END
 END
 GO
```

Listing 7-6:   A natively compiled stored procedure, `ins_native_bigtable`, to insert
              rows into the table.

Now we're going to run comparative tests for one-million row inserts into `bigtable_inmem`, via the interop and natively compiled stored procedures. We'll delete all the rows from the table before we insert the next million rows.

First, Listing 7-7 calls the interop procedure, with a parameter value of 1,000,000, outside of a user-defined transaction, so each `INSERT` in the procedure is an auto-commit transaction.

```
EXEC ins_bigtable @rows_to_INSERT = 1000000;
GO
```

Listing 7-7:   Inserting a million rows into a memory-optimized table via `ins_bigtable`.

When I executed this `EXEC` above, it took 28 seconds, as indicated in the status bar in the SQL Server Management Studio. You might want to record the amount of time it took on your SQL Server instance.

Next, Listing 7-8 calls the interop procedure inside a transaction, so that all the `INSERT` operations are a single transaction.

```
DELETE  bigtable_inmem;
GO

BEGIN TRAN
EXEC ins_bigtable @rows_to_INSERT = 1000000;
COMMIT TRAN
```

Listing 7-8:   Inserting a million rows in a single transaction.

When I executed the `EXEC` above, it took 14 seconds, which was half the time it took to insert the same number of rows in separate transactions. The savings here are primarily due to the reduction in the overhead of managing a million separate transactions.

Since this is an interop procedure, each transaction is both a regular SQL Server trans-action and an in-memory OLTP transaction, so there is a lot of overhead. The difference is not due to any additional logging, because the memory-optimized table is a SCHEMA_ONLY table and no logging is done at all.

Lastly, Listing 7-9 calls the natively compiled procedure called ins_native_bigtable with a parameter of 1,000,000.

```
DELETE bigtable_inmem;
GO
EXEC ins_native_bigtable @rows_to_INSERT = 1000000;
GO
```

Listing 7-9: Creating a natively compiled procedure and inserting a million rows.

Running this natively compiled procedure to insert the same 1,000,000 rows took only 3 seconds, less than 25% of the time it took to insert the rows through an interop procedure.

Of course, your results may vary depending on the kinds of operations you are performing; and keep in mind that I was testing this on SCHEMA_ONLY tables. For this example, I wanted to show you the impact that native compilation itself could have without interference from the overhead of disk writes that the CHECKPOINT process is doing, and any logging that the query thread would have to perform.

Performance analysis using DMV data

For more complex procedures, we will probably want to use SQL Server's DMVs to collect and analyze performance information for our procedures. The view sys.dm_exec_query_stats is one of the most commonly used tools for gathering performance infor-mation but, by default, it does not collect data from the execution of natively compiled procedures. This is because the act of gathering this internal information can slightly slow down the procedure, and natively compiled procedures were designed not to use any more CPU cycles than absolutely necessary. If you really need to gather this information and you want it to be available through sys.dm_exec_query_stats, you can run one of two stored procedures:

- **sys.sp_xtp_control_query_exec_stats** – enables **per query** statistics collection for all natively compiled stored procedures for the instance.

- **sys.sp_xtp_control_proc_exec_stats** – enables statistics collection at the procedure level, for all natively compiled stored procedures.

The syntax is shown in Listing 7-10 and the new_collection_value can be either 0 or 1, with the value 1 used to enable statistics collection.

```
EXEC sp_xtp_control_query_exec_stats [ [ @new_collection_value = ] collection_value
],[ [ @database_id = ] database_id [ , [ @xtp_object_id = ] procedure_id ]

EXEC sp_xtp_control_proc_exec_stats [ [ @new_collection_value = ] collection_value
```

Listing 7-10:   Syntax for procedures to enable statistics collection for natively compiled procedures.

As suggested, performance decreases when you enable statistics collection, but obviously collecting statistics at the procedure level with sys.sp_xtp_control_proc_exec_stats will be less expensive than using sys.sp_xtp_control_query_exec_stats to gather statistics for every query within every procedure.

If we only need to troubleshoot one, or a few, natively compiled stored procedures, there is a parameter for sys.sp_xtp_control_query_exec_stats to enable statistics collection for a single procedure, so we can run sys.sp_xtp_control_query_exec_stats once for each of those procedures.

Summary

This chapter discussed how to create **natively compiled stored procedures** to access memory-optimized tables. These procedures generate far fewer CPU instructions for the engine to execute than the equivalent interpreted T-SQL stored procedure, and can be executed directly by the CPU, without the need for further compilation or interpretation.

There are some limitations in the T-SQL constructions allowed in natively compiled procedures, and so certain transformations that the optimizer might have chosen are not supported. In addition, because of differences in the way that memory-optimized tables are organized and managed, the optimizer often needs to make different choices than it would make from a similar operation on a disk-based table. We reviewed some of the main differences.

When we access memory-optimized tables, which are also compiled, from natively compiled stored procedures, we have a highly efficient data access path, and the fastest possible query processing. We examined some Microsoft-generated performance data to get an idea of the potential size of the performance advantage to be gained from the use of natively compiled procedures, and we looked at how to run our own performance tests, and also how to collect performance diagnostic data from some Dynamic Management Views.

Additional Resources

- **Architectural Overview of SQL Server 2014's In-Memory OLTP Technology**:
  HTTP://TINYURL.COM/LPZKRAY.

- **A peek inside the in-memory OLTP engine**:
  HTTP://TINYURL.COM/Q3SB3O3.

- **Hekaton: SQL Server's Memory-Optimized OLTP Engine**
  HTTP://TINYURL.COM/LCG5M4X.

Chapter 8: SQL Server Support and Manageability

SQL Server In-Memory OLTP is an integral part of SQL Server 2014 Enterprise and Developer editions and it uses the same management tools, including SQL Server Management Studio.

Most of the standard SQL Server features work seamlessly with memory-optimized tables. This chapter will discuss feature support, including the new **Native Compilation Advisor**, which will highlight unsupported features in any stored procedures that you wish to convert to natively compiled procedures, and the Memory Optimization Advisor, which will report on unsupported features in tables that you might want to convert to memory-optimized tables. We'll then move on to discuss metrics and metadata objects added to SQL Server 2014 in order to help us manage the objects as well as track memory usage and performance, including:

- **Memory allocation, and management using Resource Governor** – a key concern when working with in-memory OLTP databases and objects.

- **Enhancements to system catalog views** – such as `sys.tables`, `sys.indexes`, and others.

- **New xtp (eXtreme Transaction Processing) Dynamic Management Objects, extended events and performance counters** – for performance monitoring and troubleshooting in-memory OLTP databases.

To round off the chapter, and the book, I'll summarize some of the key points to remember when designing efficient memory-optimized tables and indexes, and then review considerations for migrating existing tables and procedures over to SQL Server In-Memory OLTP.

Feature Support

In-memory OLTP and databases containing memory-optimized tables support much, though not all, of the SQL Server feature set. As we've seen throughout the book, SQL Server Management Studio works seamlessly with memory-optimized tables, filegroups and natively compiled procedures. In addition, we can use SQL Server Data Tools (SSDT), Server Management Objects (SMO) and PowerShell to manage our memory-optimized objects.

Database backup and restore are fully supported, as is log shipping. In terms of other "High Availability" solutions, AlwaysOn components are supported, but database mirroring and replication of memory-optimized tables are unsupported; a memory-optimized table can be a subscriber in transactional replication, but not a publisher.

In-memory OLTP feature support

For the full list of supported and unsupported features, please refer to the SQL Server In-Memory OLTP documentation: HTTP://TINYURL.COM/MUFOV2U.

In this first version of in-memory OLTP, natively compiled stored procedures support only a limited subset of the full T-SQL "surface area." Fortunately, SQL Server Management Studio for SQL Server 2014 includes a tool called **Native Compilation Advisor**, shown in Figure 8-1, which will highlight any constructs of an existing stored procedure that are incompatible with natively compiled procedures.

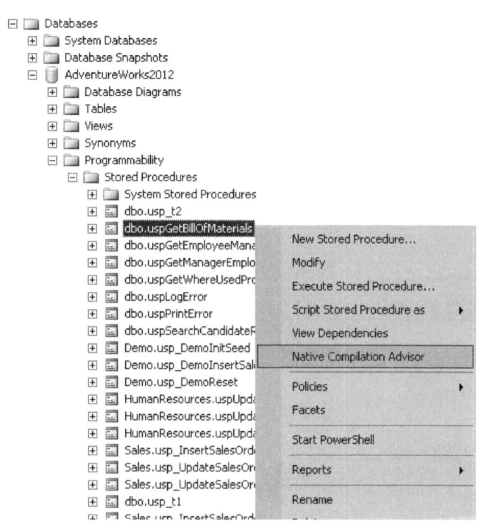

Figure 8-1: Native Compilation Advisor.

The Native Compilation Advisor will generate a list of unsupported features used in the existing procedure, and can generate a report, like the one shown in Figure 8-2.

Native Compilation Advisor evaluation results for [AdventureWorks2012].[uspGetBillOfMaterials]

Report Date/Time:4/3/2014 4:39 PM

Transact-SQL Element	Transact-SQL Code	Line Number
SET OPTION ON	SET NOCOUNT ON	2
One-part names	[BOM_cte] AS b	28
	[BOM_cte] AS cte	18
WITH clause	WITH [BOM_cte] ([ProductAssemblyID], [ComponentID], [ComponentDesc], [PerAssemblyQty], [StandardCost], [ListPrice], [BOMLevel], [RecursionLevel]) AS (SELECT b.[ProductAssemblyID], b.[ComponentID], p.[Name], b.[PerAssemblyQty], p.[StandardCost], p.[ListPrice], b.[BOMLevel], 0 FROM [Production].[BillOfMaterials] AS b INNER JOIN [Production].[Product] AS p ON b.[ComponentID] = p.[ProductID] WHERE b.[ProductAssemblyID] = @StartProductID AND @CheckDate >= b.[StartDate] AND @CheckDate <= ISNULL(b.[EndDate], @CheckDate) UNION ALL SELECT b.[ProductAssemblyID], b.[ComponentID], p.[Name], b.[PerAssemblyQty], p.[StandardCost], p.[ListPrice], b.[BOMLevel], [RecursionLevel] + 1 FROM [BOM_cte] AS cte INNER JOIN [Production].[BillOfMaterials] AS b ON b.[ProductAssemblyID] = cte.[ComponentID] INNER JOIN [Production].[Product] AS p ON b.[ComponentID] = p.[ProductID] WHERE @CheckDate >= b.[StartDate] AND @CheckDate <= ISNULL(b.[EndDate], @CheckDate))	7
	[BOM_cte] ([ProductAssemblyID], [ComponentID], [ComponentDesc], [PerAssemblyQty], [StandardCost], [ListPrice], [BOMLevel], [RecursionLevel]) AS (SELECT b.[ProductAssemblyID], b.[ComponentID], p.[Name], b.[PerAssemblyQty], p.[StandardCost], p.[ListPrice], b.[BOMLevel], 0 FROM [Production].[BillOfMaterials] AS b INNER JOIN [Production].[Product] AS p ON b.[ComponentID] = p.[ProductID] WHERE b.[ProductAssemblyID] = @StartProductID AND @CheckDate >= b.[StartDate] AND @CheckDate <= ISNULL(b.[EndDate], @CheckDate) UNION ALL SELECT b.[ProductAssemblyID], b.[ComponentID], p.[Name], b.[PerAssemblyQty], p.[StandardCost], p.[ListPrice], b.[BOMLevel], [RecursionLevel] + 1 FROM [BOM_cte] AS cte INNER JOIN [Production].[BillOfMaterials] AS b ON b.[ProductAssemblyID] = cte.[ComponentID] INNER JOIN [Production].[Product] AS p ON b.[ComponentID] = p.[ProductID] WHERE @CheckDate >= b.[StartDate] AND @CheckDate <= ISNULL(b.[EndDate], @CheckDate))	7
UNION	SELECT b.[ProductAssemblyID], b.[ComponentID], p.[Name], b.[PerAssemblyQty], p.[StandardCost], p.[ListPrice], b.[BOMLevel], 0 FROM [Production].[BillOfMaterials] AS b INNER JOIN [Production].[Product] AS p ON b.[ComponentID] = p.[ProductID] UNION ALL	9
MAX RECURSION	MAXRECURSION 25	31

Figure 8-2: Native Compilation Advisor report.

Another feature, that works similarly to the Native Compilation Advisor, is the **Memory Optimization Advisor**, available from SQL Server Management Studio 2014 when you right-click on a disk-based table. This tool will report on table features that are unsupported, such as LOB columns, and IDENTITY columns with increment other than 1. This tool will also provide information such as the estimated memory requirement for the table if it is converted to be memory optimized. Finally, the Memory Optimization Advisor can actually convert the table to a memory-optimized table, as long as it doesn't contain unsupported features.

Memory Allocation and Management

When running in-memory OLTP, we need to configure SQL Server with sufficient memory to hold all memory-optimized tables. Failure to allocate sufficient memory will cause transactions to fail at runtime during any operations that require additional memory. Normally this would happen during INSERT or UPDATE operations. However, it could also happen for DELETE operations on a memory-optimized table with range indexes because, as we discussed when describing Bw-trees in Chapter 4, a DELETE can cause a page merge, and since SQL Server never updates index pages, the merge operation will allocate new pages.

If this happens, and you're not able to increase the amount of memory available to SQL Server, you may be forced to drop some of the memory-optimized tables to free up memory space. This is why it's so important to understand your memory allocation requirements for memory-optimized tables before beginning to migrate them.

Fully integrated with the SQL Server memory manager is the **in-memory OLTP memory manager**, which will react to memory pressure when possible, by becoming more aggressive in cleaning up old row versions.

The maximum amount of memory available for memory-optimized tables is determined by the maximum number of checkpoint files that are supported and, for a single database, that number is 4,000. Since each file is 128 MB, that gives a theoretical memory limit of 512 GB for memory-optimized tables in a single database. However, in order to guarantee that SQL Server can keep up with merging checkpoint files, with no risk of hitting the limit of 4,000 files, in-memory OLTP supports a maximum for memory-optimized tables of 256 GB of memory per database.

When working with SQL Server In-Memory OLTP, remember that it is not necessary that the whole database fits in memory; we can work with disk-based tables, right alongside memory-optimized tables.

When trying to predict the amount of memory required for memory-optimized tables, a rule of thumb is to allow two times the amount of memory needed for the data. Beyond this, the total memory requirement depends on the workload; if there are a lot of data modifications due to OLTP operations, you'll need more memory for the row versions. If the workload comprises mainly reading existing data, there might be less memory required.

Planning space requirements for hash indexes is straightforward. Each bucket requires 8 bytes, so the memory required is simply the number of buckets times 8 bytes. Planning space for range indexes is slightly trickier. The size for a range index depends on both the size of the index key and the number of rows in the table. We can assume each index row is 8 bytes plus the size of the index key (assume K bytes), so the maximum number of rows that fit on a page would be **8176 / (K+8)**. Divide that result into the expected number of rows to get an initial estimate. Remember that not all index pages are 8 KB, and not all pages are completely full. As SQL Server needs to split and merge pages, it will need to create new pages and we need to allow space for them, until the garbage collection process removes them.

Using Resource Governor for memory management

In SQL Server 2014, we can use SQL Server Resource Governor to manage memory allocation for in-memory databases and objects. We can *bind* one or more databases to a resource pool, assign to the pool the required amount of memory, and that will be the maximum amount of memory available to memory-optimized objects in those databases. In order to ensure that the system remains stable under memory pressure, there is a hard limit of 80% of your SQL Server instance's maximum memory that can be assigned to a resource pool.

In fact, Resource Governor manages all memory consumed by memory-optimized tables and their indexes. If we don't map a database to a pool explicitly, then SQL Server will map it implicitly to the default pool.

The first step is to create a resource pool for the in-memory OLTP database, specifying a MIN_MEMORY_PERCENT and MAX_MEMORY_PERCENT of the same value. This specifies the percentage of the SQL Server memory which may be allocated to memory-optimized tables in databases associated with this pool. Listing 8-1, for example, creates a resource pool called HkPool and allocates to it 50% of available memory.

```
CREATE RESOURCE POOL HkPool
WITH (MIN_MEMORY_PERCENT=50,
      MAX_MEMORY_PERCENT=50);
ALTER RESOURCE GOVERNOR RECONFIGURE;
```

Listing 8-1:   Create a resource pool for a database containing memory-optimized tables.

Next, we need to bind the databases that we wish to manage to their respective pools, using the procedure **sp_xtp_bind_db_resource_pool**. Note that one pool may contain many databases, but a database is only associated with one pool at any point in time.

```
EXEC sp_xtp_bind_db_resource_pool 'HkDB', 'HkPool';
```

Listing 8-2:   Binding a database to a resource pool.

SQL Server assigns memory to a resource pool as it is allocated, so simply associating a database with a pool will not transfer the assignment of any memory already allocated via the previous pool. In order to "activate" the binding to the new pool, we need to take the database offline and bring it back online, as shown in Listing 83. As SQL Server reads data into the memory-optimized tables, it will associate the memory with the new pool.

```
ALTER DATABASE [HkDB] SET OFFLINE;
ALTER DATABASE [HkDB] SET ONLINE;
GO
```

Listing 8-3:   Taking a database offline and then online to allow memory to be associated with the new resource pool.

We can remove the binding between a database and a pool using the procedure
`sp_xtp_unbind_db_resource_pool`, as shown in Listing 8-4. For example, we
may wish to move the database to a different pool, or to delete the pool entirely, to
replace it with some other pool or pools.

```
EXEC sp_xtp_unbind_db_resource_pool 'HkDB';
```

Listing 8-4: Remove the binding between a database and a resource pool.

Memory usage report

A new report available through SQL Server Management Studio will provide an instant
snapshot of the current memory used by memory-optimized tables and their indexes. In
Object Explorer, simply right-click the appropriate database, select **Reports | Standard
Reports | Memory Usage By Memory Optimized Objects**.

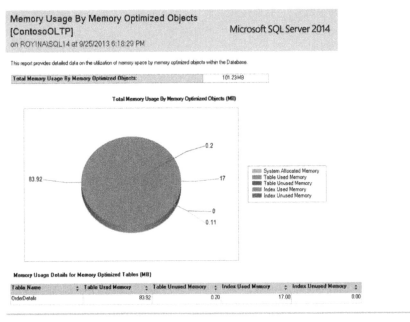

Figure 8-3: Report of memory usage by memory optimized objects.

This report shows you the space used by the table rows and the indexes, as well as the small amount of space used by the system. Remember that hash indexes will have memory allocated for the declared number of buckets as soon as they're created, so this report will show memory usage for those indexes before any rows are inserted. For range indexes, memory will not be allocated until rows are added, and the memory requirement will depend on the size of the index keys and the number of rows, as discussed previously.

Metadata Enhancements and Additions

SQL Server 2014 introduces enhancements to existing metadata objects to provide information about memory-optimized tables and procedures. In addition, there is one new catalog view for memory-optimized tables, and several new dynamic management objects, some of which have been discussed in earlier chapters.

One property function, OBJECTPROPERTY, has been enhanced to include a property called TableIsMemoryOptimized.

Catalog view enhancements

The following system views have been enhanced:

- **sys.tables** – has three new columns:

  - durability (0 or 1)

  - durability_desc (SCHEMA_AND_DATA and SCHEMA_ONLY)

  - is_memory_optimized (0 or 1).

- **sys.table_types** – now has a column is_memory_optimized.

- **sys.indexes** – now has a possible type value of 7 and a corresponding `type_desc` value of NONCLUSTERED HASH. (Range indexes have a `type_value` of 2 and a `type_desc` of NONCLUSTERED, just as for a non-clustered B-tree index).

- **sys.index_columns** – now has different semantics for the column `is_descending_key`, in that for HASH indexes the value is meaningless and ignored.

- **sys.data_spaces** – now has a possible type value of FX and a corresponding `type_desc` value of MEMORY_OPTIMIZED_DATA_FILEGROUP.

- **sys.sql_modules** and **sys.all_sql_modules** – now contain a column `uses_native_compilation`.

As a simple example, the query in Listing 8-5 reports which databases a SQL Server instance could support memory-optimized tables on, based on the requirement of having a memory-optimized filegroup that contains at least one file. It uses the procedure `sp_MSforeachdb` to loop through all databases, and print a message for each database that meets the requirements.

```
EXEC sp_MSforeachdb 'USE ? IF EXISTS (SELECT 1 FROM sys.filegroups FG
              JOIN sys.database_files F
                        ON FG.data_space_id = F.data_space_id
      WHERE FG.type = ''FX'' AND F.type = 2)
              PRINT ''?'' + '' can contain memory-optimized tables.'' ';
GO
```

Listing 8-5: Report which databases support creation of memory-optimized tables.

A new catalog view, **sys.hash_indexes**, has been added to support hash indexes. This view is based on **sys.indexes**, so it has the same columns as that view, with one extra column added. The `bucket_count` column shows a count of the number of hash buckets specified for the index and the value cannot be changed without dropping and recreating the index.

In addition, there are several new dynamic management objects that provide information specifically for memory-optimized tables.

Dynamic Management Objects

The following SQL Server Dynamic Management Objects, a few of which we've used previously in the book, are new for in-memory OLTP. (As mentioned earlier, the xtp identifier stands for eXtreme Transaction Processing.) The ones that start with sys.dm_db_xtp_* give information about individual in-memory OLTP-enabled databases, and the ones that start with sys.dm_xtp_* provide instance-wide information. You can read about the details of these objects in the documentation, but a brief description is provided here.

- **sys.dm_db_xtp_checkpoint_stats**
  Returns statistics about the in-memory OLTP checkpoint operations in the current database. If the database has no in-memory OLTP objects, returns an empty result set.

- **sys.dm_db_xtp_checkpoint_files**
  Displays information about checkpoint files, including file size, physical location and the transaction ID. For the current checkpoint that has not closed, the state column of this DMV will display UNDER CONSTRUCTION, for new files. A checkpoint closes automatically when the transaction log grows 512 MB since the last checkpoint, or if you issue the CHECKPOINT command.

- **sys.dm_xtp_merge_requests**
  Tracks database merge requests. The merge request may have been generated by SQL Server or the request could have been made by a user, with sys.sp_xtp_merge_checkpoint_files.

- **sys.dm_xtp_gc_stats**
  Provides information about the current behavior of the in-memory OLTP garbage collection process. The parallel_assist_count represents the number of rows processed by user transactions and the idle_worker_count represents the rows processed by the idle worker.

- **sys.dm_xtp_gc_queue_stats**
  Provides details of activity on each garbage collection worker queue on the server (one queue per logical CPU). As described in Chapter 5, the garbage collection thread adds "work items" to this queue, consisting of groups of "stale" rows, eligible for garbage collection. By taking regular snapshots of these queue lengths, we can make sure garbage collection is keeping up with the demand. If the queue lengths remain steady, garbage collection is keeping up. If the queue lengths are growing over time, this is an indication that garbage collection is falling behind (and you may need to allocate more memory).

- **sys.dm_db_xtp_gc_cycle_stats**
  For the current database, outputs a ring buffer of garbage collection cycles containing up to 1024 rows (each row represents a single cycle). As discussed in Chapter 5, to spread out the garbage collection work, the garbage collection thread arranges transactions into "generations" according to when they committed compared to the oldest active transaction. They are grouped into units of 16 transactions across 16 generations as follows:

  - **Generation 0**: Stores all transactions that have committed earlier than the oldest active transaction and therefore the row versions generated by them can be immediately garbage collected.

  - **Generations 1-14**: Store transactions with a timestamp greater than the oldest active transaction meaning that the row versions can't yet be garbage collected. Each generation can hold up to 16 transactions. A total of 224 (14 * 16) transactions can exist in these generations.

  - **Generation 15**: Stores the remainder of the transactions with a timestamp greater than the oldest active transaction. Similar to generation 0, there is no limit to the number of transactions in Generation 15.

- **sys.dm_db_xtp_hash_index_stats**
Provides information on the number of buckets and hash chain lengths for hash indexes on a table, useful for understanding and tuning the bucket counts (see Chapter 4). If there are large tables in your database, queries against **sys.dm_db_xtp_hash_index_stats** may take a long time since it needs to scan the entire table.

- **sys.dm_db_xtp_nonclustered_index_stats**
Provides information about consolidation, split, and merge operations on the Bw-tree indexes.

- **sys.dm_db_xtp_index_stats**
Contains statistics about index accesses collected since the last database restart. Provides details of expired rows eligible for garbage collection, detected during index scans (see Chapter 5).

- **sys.dm_db_xtp_object_stats**
Provides information about the write conflicts and unique constraint violations on memory-optimized tables.

- **sys.dm_xtp_system_memory_consumers**
Reports system-level memory consumers for in-memory OLTP. The memory for these consumers comes either from the default pool (when the allocation is in the context of a user thread) or from the internal pool (if the allocation is in the context of a system thread).

- **sys.dm_db_xtp_table_memory_stats**
Returns memory usage statistics for each in-memory OLTP table (user and system) in the current database. The system tables have negative object IDs and are used to store runtime information for the in-memory OLTP engine. Unlike user objects, system tables are internal and only exist in memory, therefore they are not visible through catalog views. System tables are used to store information such as metadata for all data/delta files in storage, merge requests, watermarks for delta files to filter rows, dropped tables, and relevant information for recovery and backups. Given that the in-memory OLTP engine can have up to 8,192 data and delta file pairs, for large in-memory databases the memory taken by system tables can be a few megabytes.

- **sys.dm_db_xtp_memory_consumers**
  Reports the database-level memory consumers in the in-memory OLTP database engine. The view returns a row for each memory consumer that the engine uses.

- **sys.dm_xtp_transaction_stats**
  Reports accumulated statistics about transactions that have run since the server started.

- **sys.dm_db_xtp_transactions**
  Reports the active transactions in the in-memory OLTP database engine (covered in Chapter 5).

- **sys.dm_xtp_threads** (undocumented, for internal use only).
  Reports on the performance of the garbage collection threads, whether they are user threads or a dedicated garbage collection thread.

- **sys.dm_xtp_transaction_recent_rows** (undocumented, for internal use only).
  Provides information that allows the in-memory OLTP database engine to perform its validity and dependency checks during post processing.

Extended events

The in-memory OLTP engine provides three extended event packages to help in monitoring and troubleshooting. Listing 8-6 reveals the package names and the number of events in each package.

```
SELECT   p.name AS PackageName ,
         COUNT(*) AS NumberOfEvents
FROM     sys.dm_xe_objects o
         JOIN sys.dm_xe_packages p ON o.package_guid = p.guid
WHERE    p.name LIKE 'Xtp%'
GROUP BY p.name;
GO
```

Listing 8-6:   Retrieve package information for in-memory OLTP extended events.

My results show three packages, **XtpCompile** (6 xEvents), **XtpRuntime** (119 xEvents) and **XtpEngine** (10 xEvents).

Listing 8-7 returns the names of all the extended events currently available in the in-memory OLTP packages.

```
SELECT   p.name AS PackageName ,
         o.name AS EventName ,
         o.description AS EventDescription
FROM     sys.dm_xe_objects o
         JOIN sys.dm_xe_packages p ON o.package_guid = p.guid
WHERE    p.name LIKE 'Xtp%';
GO
```

Listing 8-7:   Retrieve the names of the in-memory OLTP extended events.

Performance counters

The in-memory OLTP engine provides performance counters to help in monitoring and troubleshooting. Listing 8-8 returns the performance counters currently available.

```
SELECT   object_name AS ObjectName ,
         counter_name AS CounterName
FROM     sys.dm_os_performance_counters
WHERE    object_name LIKE 'XTP%';
GO
```

Listing 8-8:   Retrieve the names of the in-memory OLTP performance counters.

My results show 51 counters in six different categories. The categories are listed and described in Table 8-1.

Performance Counter	Description
XTP Cursors	Contains counters related to internal XTP engine cursors. Cursors are the low-level building blocks that the XTP engine uses to process T-SQL queries. As such, you do not typically have direct control over them.
XTP Garbage Collection	Contains counters related to the XTP engine's garbage collector. Counters include the number of rows processed, the number of scans per second, and the number of rows expired per second.
XTP Phantom Processor	Contains counters related to the XTP engine's phantom processing subsystem. This component is responsible for detecting phantom rows in transactions running at the SERIALIZABLE isolation level.
XTP Storage	Contains counters related to the checkpoint files. Counters include the number of checkpoints closed, and the number of files merged.
XTP Transaction Log	Contains counters related to XTP transaction logging in SQL Server. Counters include the number of log bytes and the number of log records per second written by the in-memory OLTP engine.
XTP Transactions	Contains counters related to XTP engine transactions in SQL Server. Counters include the number of commit dependencies taken and the number of commit dependencies that have been rolled back.

Table 8-1:   Categories of performance counters for in-memory OLTP processing.

Best Practices for Designing Memory-optimized Tables and Indexes

We've discussed best practice recommendations throughout the book, and this section is really just a recap of some of the most important ones. Keep these principles in mind as you design your memory-optimized tables and indexes.

- Use the `COLLATE` clause at the column level, specifying the `BIN2` collation for every character column in a table you want to memory-optimize, rather than the database level, because use at the database level will affect every table and every column in a database. Or, specify the `COLLATE` clause in your queries, where it can be used for any comparison, sorting, or grouping operation.

- Do not over- or underestimate the bucket count for hash indexes if at all possible. The bucket could should be at least equal to the number of distinct values for the index key columns.

- For very low cardinality columns, create range indexes instead of hash indexes.

- Statistics are not updated automatically, and there are no automatic recompiles of any queries on memory-optimized tables.

- Memory-optimized table variables behave the same as regular table variables, but are stored in your database's memory space, not in `tempdb`. You can consider using memory-optimized table variables anywhere, as they are not transactional and can help relieve `tempdb` contention.

One important difference to keep in mind when creating a memory-optimized table variable is that it must be based on a memory-optimized table type. Table types can be created for disk-based tables as well, but are not required for disk-based table variables. Listing 8-9 creates a memory-optimized table variable, built using a memory-optimized table type (based on a table definition in the `AdventureWorks2014` in-memory OLTP sample database). Note that, just like memory-optimized tables, memory-optimized table variables must be defined with at least one index.

```
USE HKDB;
CREATE TYPE SalesOrderDetailType_inmem
AS TABLE
(
  OrderQty smallint NOT NULL,
  ProductID int NOT NULL,
  SpecialOfferID int NOT NULL,
  LocalID int NOT NULL,

  INDEX IX_ProductID  NONCLUSTERED HASH (ProductID) WITH (BUCKET_COUNT = 131072),
  INDEX IX_SpecialOfferID NONCLUSTERED (SpecialOfferID)
)
WITH (MEMORY_OPTIMIZED = ON );
GO
DECLARE @SalesDetail SalesOrderDetailType_inmem;
GO
```

Listing 8-9:   Creating a memory-optimized table variable using a memory-optimized table type.

In-memory OLTP is still a new technology and, as of this writing, there are only a few applications using memory-optimized tables in a production environment (later in the chapter, I list a few such applications). As more and more applications are deployed and monitored, best practices will be discovered.

Migrating to SQL Server In-Memory OLTP

Although in-memory OLTP might sound like a panacea for all your relational database performance problems, it isn't, of course. There are some applications that can experience enormous improvement when using memory-optimized tables and natively compiled stored procedures, and others that will see no drastic gains, or perhaps no gains at all.

Common application bottlenecks that in-memory OLTP can resolve

The kinds of application that will achieve the best improvements are the ones that are currently experiencing the bottlenecks that in-memory OLTP addresses and removes.

In-memory OLTP addresses the major bottlenecks below.

- **Lock or latch contention**
  The lock- and latch-free design of memory-optimized tables is probably the best-known performance benefit. As discussed in detail in earlier chapters, the data structures used for the memory-optimized tables' row versions mean that SQL Server can preserve ACID transaction properties without the need to acquire locks. Also, the fact that the rows are not stored within pages in memory buffers means that there is no latching. This allow for high concurrency data access and modification without the need for locks or latches. Tables used by an application showing excessive lock or latch wait times will likely show substantial performance improvement when migrated to in-memory OLTP.

- **I/O and logging**
  Data rows in a memory-optimized table are always in memory, so no disk reads are ever required to make the data available. The streaming checkpoint operations are also highly optimized to use minimal resources to write the durable data to disk in the checkpoint files. In addition, in-memory OLTP never writes index information to disk, reducing the I/O requirements even further. If an application shows excessive page I/O latch waits, or any other waits associated with reading from, or writing to, disk, use of memory-optimized tables will likely improve performance.

- **Transaction logging**
  Log I/O can be another bottleneck with disk-based tables since, in most cases for OLTP operations, SQL Server writes to the transaction log on disk a separate log record describing every table and index row modification. In-memory OLTP allows us to create SCHEMA_ONLY tables that do not require any logging, but even for tables

defined as SCHEMA_AND_DATA, the logging overhead is significantly reduced. Each log record for changes to a memory-optimized table can contain information about many modified rows, and changes to indexes are never logged at all. If an application experiences high wait times due to log writes, migrating the most heavily-modified tables to memory-optimized tables is likely to result in performance improvements.

- **Hardware resource limitations**
In addition to the limits on disk I/O that can cause performance problems with disk-based tables, other hardware resources can also be the cause of bottlenecks. CPU resources are frequently stressed in compute-intensive OLTP workloads. In addition, CPU resources also cause slowdowns when small queries need to be executed repeatedly and the interpretation of the code needed by these queries needs to be repeated over and over again. Migrating such code to natively compiled procedures can greatly reduce the CPU resources required, because the natively compiled code can perform the same operations with far fewer CPU instructions than the interpreted code. If you have many small code blocks running repeatedly, especially if you are noticing a high number of recompiles, you may notice a substantial performance improvement from migrating this code into natively compiled procedures.

Application requirements compatible with migration to in-memory OLTP

The following sections will describe some of the most common data access and manipulation scenarios that often lead to the application bottlenecks described.

High volume of INSERTs

Applications that execute high volumes of INSERTs, such as sales order entry systems, frequently encounter bottlenecks on attempting to acquire locks and latches on the last page of a table or index, in cases where the application needs to INSERT the rows in a particular order. Even if row locks are being used, there are still latches acquired on the page, and for very high volumes this can be problematic. Also, the logging required for the inserted rows and for the index rows created for each inserted data row can cause performance degradation, if the INSERT volume is high.

SQL Server In-Memory OLTP addresses these problems by eliminating the need for locks and latches. Logging overhead is reduced because operations on memory-optimized tables log their changes more efficiently. In addition, the changes to the indexes are not logged at all. If the application is such that the INSERT operations initially load data into a staging table, then creating the staging table to be SCHEMA_ONLY will also remove any overhead associated with logging the table rows.

Finally, the code to process the INSERTs must be run repeatedly for each row inserted, and when using interop T-SQL this imposes a lot of overhead. If the code to process the INSERTs meets the criteria for creating a natively compiled procedure, executing the INSERTs through compiled code can improve performance dramatically, as demonstrated in Chapter 7.

High volume of SELECTs

An application needing to process a high volume of SELECT operations quickly, and to be able to scale to support even greater numbers, faces the same locking and latching bottlenecks as in the previous example (of course, there is no logging requirement) and, similarly, migration to in-memory OLTP could offer performance benefits.

Bear in mind, however, that the assumption here is of a typical OTLP workload consisting of many concurrent SELECTs, each reading a small amount of data. If your workload consists of SELECTs that each process a large number of rows, then this is more problematical, since operations on memory-optimized tables are always executed on a single thread; there is no support for parallel operations.

If you do have datasets that would benefit from parallelism, you can consider moving the relevant data to a separate disk-based table, where the query optimizer can consider use of parallelism. Potentially, however, the mere act of separating the data into its own table may reduce the number of rows that need to be scanned to the point where that table becomes viable for migration to in-memory OLTP. If the code for processing these rows can be executed in a natively compiled procedure, the speed improvement for compiled code can sometimes outweigh the cost of having to run the queries single threaded.

CPU-intensive operations

A common requirement is to load large volumes of data, as discussed previously, but then to process the data in some way, before it is available for reading by the application. This processing can involve updating or deleting some of the data, if it is deemed inappropriate, or it can involve computations to put the data into the proper form for use.

The biggest bottleneck that the application will encounter in this case is the locking and latching as the data is read for processing, and then the CPU resources required once processing is invoked, which will vary depending on the complexity of the code executed.

As discussed, in-memory OLTP can provide a solution for all of these bottlenecks.

Extremely fast business transactions

Applications that need to run a large volume of simple transactions very quickly, supporting hundreds if not thousands of concurrent users, experience both latching and locking bottlenecks as well as CPU bottlenecks associated with the query processing stack. If the queries themselves are relatively short and simple, the cost of repeated recompilation and query interpretation can become a major component of the overall processing time.

In-memory OLTP solves these problems by providing a lock- and latch-free environment. Also, the ability to run the code in a truly compiled form, with no compiling or interpretation, can give an enormous performance boost for these kinds of applications.

Session state management

Session state management, a function required by many different types of application, involves maintaining state information across various boundaries, where normally there is no communication. The most prominent example is web-based interactions using HTTP. When users connect to a website, the web application needs to maintain information about their choices and actions across multiple HTTP requests.

In general, we can maintain this state information in the database system, but typically at a high cost. The state information is usually very dynamic, with each user's information changing very frequently, and with the need to maintain state for multiple concurrent users. It also can involve lookup queries for each user to gather other information the system might be keeping for that user, such as past activity. Although the data maintained might be minimal in size, the number of requests to access that data can be large, leading to extreme locking and latching requirements, and resulting in very noticeable bottlenecks and serious slowdowns in responses to user requests.

In-memory OLTP is the perfect solution for this application requirement, since a small memory-optimized table can handle an enormous number of concurrent lookups and modifications. In addition, a session state table is almost always transient and does not need to be preserved across server restarts, so a **SCHEMA_ONLY** table can be used to improve the performance even further.

Unsuitable application requirements

Although there are many types of application that can gain considerable performance improvement when using in-memory OLTP, either just by creating memory-optimized tables or by including natively compiled stored procedures, some applications have requirements and characteristics that make them unsuitable for migration to in-memory OLTP.

In most cases, at least part of any application could be better served using traditional disk-based tables, or you might not see any improvement with in-memory OLTP. If your application meets any of the following criteria, you may need to reconsider whether in-memory OLTP is the right choice.

- **Inability to make changes**
  If an application requires table features that are not supported by memory-optimized tables, you will not be able to create in-memory tables without first redefining the table structure. In addition, if the application code for accessing and manipulating the table data uses constructs not supported for natively compiled procedures, you may have to limit your T-SQL to using only interop code.

- **Memory limitations**
  Memory-optimized tables must reside completely in memory. If the size of the tables exceeds what SQL Server In-Memory OLTP or a particular machine supports, you will not be able to have all the required data in memory. Of course, you can have some memory-optimized tables and some disk-based tables, but you'll need to analyze the workload carefully to identify those tables that will benefit most from migration to memory-optimized tables.

- **Non-OLTP workload**
  In-memory OLTP, as the name implies, is designed to be of most benefit to Online Transaction Processing operations. It may offer benefits to other types of processing, such as reporting and data warehousing, but those are not the design goals of the feature. If you are working with processing that is not OLTP in nature, you should carefully test all operations to verify that in-memory OLTP provides measurable improvements.

- **Dependencies on locking behavior**
  Some applications rely on specific locking behavior, supplied with pessimistic concurrency on disk-based tables. It's not a best practice, in most cases, because this locking behavior can change between SQL Server releases, but it does happen. For example, an application might use the **READPAST** hint to manage work queues, which requires SQL Server to use locks in order to find the next row in the queue to process. Alternatively, let's say the application is written to expect the behavior delivered by accessing disk-based tables using **SNAPSHOT** isolation. In the event of a write-write conflict, the correct functioning of the application code may rely on the expectation that SQL Server will not report the conflict until the first process commits. This expected behavior is incompatible with that delivered by the use of **SNAPSHOT** isolation with memory-optimized tables (the standard isolation level when accessing memory-optimized tables). If an application relies on specific locking behavior, then you'll need to delay converting to in-memory OLTP until you can rewrite the relevant sections of your code.

Current applications

As noted earlier, there are currently relatively few applications using memory-optimized tables in a production environment, but the list is growing rapidly. When considering a migration, you might want to review the published information regarding the types of application that are already benefiting from running SQL Server In-Memory OLTP. For example (the URLs refer to Microsoft case studies):

- **bwin** (HTTP://TINYURL.COM/LTYA25M), the world's largest regulated online gaming company. SQL Server 2014 allows bwin to scale its applications to 250 K requests a second, a 16x increase from before, and to provide an overall faster and smoother customer playing experience.

- **Ferranti** (HTTP://TINYURL.COM/OZSCND4), which provides solutions for the energy market worldwide, is collecting large amounts of data using smart metering. They use in-memory OLTP to help utilities be more efficient by allowing them to switch from the traditional meter that is measured once a month to smart meters that provide usage measurements every 15 minutes. By taking more measurements, they can better match supply to demand. With the new system supported by SQL Server 2014, they increased from 5 million transactions a month to 500 million a day.

- **TPP** (HTTP://TINYURL.COM/Q49J6WQ), a clinical software provider, is managing more than 30 million patient records. With in-memory OLTP, they were able to get their new solution up and running in half a day, and their application is now seven times faster than before, peaking at about 34,700 transactions per second.

- **SBI Liquidity Market** (HTTP://TINYURL.COM/KOKHOLS), an online services provider for foreign currency exchange (FX) trading, wanted to increase the capacity of its trading platform to support its growing business and expansion worldwide. SBI Liquidity Market is now achieving better scalability and easier management with in-memory OLTP and expects to strengthen its competitive advantage with a trading platform that is ready to take on the global marketplace.

- **Edgenet** (HTTP://TINYURL.COM/LNRLS4U) provides optimized product data for suppliers, retailers, and search engines including Bing and Google. They implemented SQL Server 2014 to deliver accurate inventory data to customers. They are now experiencing seven time faster throughput and their users are creating reports with Microsoft's self-service Business Intelligence tools to model huge data volumes in seconds.

The migration process

SQL Server In-Memory OLTP can make migration a very straightforward and manageable process, because migration doesn't have to be an all-or-nothing decision. Since you can access memory-optimized tables with interpreted T-SQL as well as with natively compiled stored procedures, and access both memory-optimized tables and disk-based tables in the same query, it means that you can migrate a database to an in-memory OLTP environment gradually and iteratively.

You could choose to just convert one or two critical tables that experience an excessive number of locks or latches, or long durations on waits for locks or latches, or both. Convert tables before stored procedures, since natively compiled procedures will only be able to access memory-optimized tables.

Workload analysis and baselining

Ideally, before migrating any tables or stored procedures to use in-memory OLTP, you need to perform a thorough analysis of your current workload, and establish a baseline.

More on monitoring, analysis and baselining

Coverage of these topics is well beyond the scope of this book, but you can take a look at this page in the SQL Server 2014 documentation to get several pointers on performance this kind of analysis: HTTP://TINYURL.COM/NZZET9B.

Consider the following list of steps as a guide, as you work through a migration to in-memory OLTP:

1. Capture baseline performance metrics running queries against existing tables.

2. Identify the tables with the biggest bottlenecks.

3. Address the constructs in the table DDLs that are not supported for memory-optimized tables. The Memory Optimization Advisor can tell you what constructs are unsupported for memory-optimized tables.

4. Recreate the tables as in-memory, to be accessed using interop code.

5. Identify any procedures, or sections of code, which experience performance bottlenecks when accessing the converted tables.

6. Address the T-SQL limitations in the code. If the code is in a stored procedure, you can use the Native Compilation Advisor. Recreate the code in a natively compiled procedure.

7. Compare performance against the baseline.

You can think of this as a cyclical process. Start with a few tables and convert them, then convert the most critical procedures that access those tables, convert a few more tables, and then a couple more procedures. You can repeat this cycle as needed, until you reach the point where the performance gains are minimal.

You can also consider using a tool called Analysis, Migration and Reporting (AMR), provided with SQL Server 2014, to help with the performance analysis prior to migrating to in-memory OLTP.

Using the AMR tool

Assuming you elected to include the complete set of management tools during the installation process, the AMR tool mentioned above will provide recommendations on the tables and procedures that may benefit most from migrating to in-memory OLTP.

AMR uses Management Data Warehouse (MDW) using the data collector, and produces reports which we can access by right-clicking on the MDW database, and choosing **Reports | Management Data Warehouse**. You will then have the option to choose **Transaction Performance Analysis Overview**.

One of the reports will describe which tables are prime candidates for conversion to memory-optimized tables, as well as providing an estimate of the size of the effort required to perform the conversion, based on how many unsupported features the table concurrently uses. For example, it will point out unsupported data types and constraints used in the table.

Another report will contain recommendations on which procedures might benefit from being converted to natively compiled procedures for use with memory-optimized tables.

Based on recommendations from the MDW reports, you can start converting tables into memory-optimized tables one at a time, starting with the ones that would benefit most from the memory-optimized structures. As you start seeing the benefit of the conversion to memory-optimized tables, you can continue to convert more of your tables, but access them using your normal T-SQL interface, with very few application changes.

Once your tables have been converted, you can then start planning a rewrite of the code into natively compiled stored procedures, again starting with the ones that the MDW reports indicate would provide the most benefit.

Summary

Using SQL Server In-Memory OLTP, we can create and work with tables that are memory-optimized and extremely efficient to manage, often providing performance optimization for OLTP workloads. They are accessed with true multi-version optimistic concurrency control requiring no locks or latches during processing. All in-memory OLTP memory-optimized tables must have at least one index, and all access is via indexes. In-memory OLTP memory-optimized tables can be referenced in the same transactions as disk-based tables, with only a few restrictions. Natively compiled stored procedures are the fastest way to access your memory-optimized tables and performance business logic computations.

If most, or all, of an application's data is able to be entirely memory resident, the costing rules that the SQL Server optimizer has used since the very first version become almost completely obsolete, because the rules assume all pages accessed can potentially require a physical read from disk. If there is no reading from disk required, the optimizer can use a different costing algorithm. In addition, if there is no wait time required for disk reads, other wait statistics (such as waiting for locks to be released, waiting for latches to be available, or waiting for log writes to complete) can become disproportionately large. In-memory OLTP addresses all these issues. It removes the issues involved in waiting for locks to be released, using a new type of multi-version optimistic concurrency control. It also reduces the delays of waiting for log writes by generating far less log data, and needing fewer log writes.

Additional Resources

- **Managing Memory for In-Memory OLTP**:
  HTTP://TINYURL.COM/LOYTZAJ.

- **Using the Resource Governor** – extensive white paper written when the feature was introduced in SQL Server 2008:
  HTTP://BIT.LY/1SHHAPQ.

- **Resource Governor in SQL Server 2012** – covers significant changes in this release:
  HTTP://TINYURL.COM/MZJRNLO.

- **Extended Events** – the best place to get a start on working with extended events is in the SQL Server documentation:
  HTTP://TINYURL.COM/LMHGD5S.

- **Common Workload Patterns and Migration Considerations** – types of bottlenecks and workloads that are most suited to in-memory OLTP:
  HTTP://TINYURL.COM/KKYRGEO.

- **Transact-SQL Constructs Not Supported by In-Memory OLTP** – recommended workarounds for the current limitations in support for the T-SQL surface:
  HTTP://TINYURL.COM/M7O4GD4.

Index

W

About Red Gate

You know those annoying jobs that spoil your day whenever they come up?

Writing out scripts to update your production database, or trawling through code to see why it's running so slow.

Red Gate makes tools to fix those problems for you. Many of our tools are now industry standards. In fact, at the last count, we had over 650,000 users.

But we try to go beyond that. We want to support you and the rest of the SQL Server and .NET communities in any way we can.

First, we publish a library of free books on .NET and SQL Server. You're reading one of them now. You can get dozens more from www.red-gate.com/books

Second, we commission and edit rigorously accurate articles from experts on the front line of application and database development. We publish them in our online journal Simple Talk, which is read by millions of technology professionals each year.

On SQL Server Central, we host the largest SQL Server community in the world. As well as lively forums, it puts out a daily dose of distilled SQL Server know-how through its newsletter, which now has nearly a million subscribers (and counting).

Third, we organize and sponsor events (about 50,000 of you came to them last year), including SQL in the City, a free event for SQL Server users in the US and Europe.

So, if you want more free books and articles, or to get sponsorship, or to try some tools that make your life easier, then head over to www.red-gate.com.